Gleaned from her personal diaries, *Awakening to Sacred Presence* is beautifully written, spiritually luminous, a poetic testament to God's transforming love. Readers will find Doreen Kostynuik to be an endearing and trustworthy guide in the struggle toward inner freedom. I highly recommend this work to anyone seeking spiritual truth and healing.

-Mark Yaconelli, author of *The Gift of Hard Things* and *Between the Listening and the Telling How Stories Can Save Us*

Doreen's writing is powerful and evocative. I felt the entire gamut of emotions reading part one of her manuscript. Her personal stories are filled with imagery and I could see her at different stages of her life's journey, in my mind's eye. I appreciate how open and vulnerable she has been in her memoir, which calls upon the reader to reflect on one's own life in an equally honest manner.

-Char deFaye, Secondary English teacher.

# Awakening to Sacred Presence:

## The Way of Wholeness and Holiness

BY

DOREEN D. KOSTYNUIK

◆ FriesenPress

One Printers Way
Altona, MB R0G 0B0
Canada

www.friesenpress.com

ISBN
978-1-03-918975-1 (Hardcover)
978-1-03-918974-4 (Paperback)
978-1-03-918976-8 (eBook)

*1. RELIGION, INSPIRATIONAL*

Distributed to the trade by The Ingram Book Company

# TABLE OF CONTENTS

*Though the Lord may give you the bread of adversity
and the water of affliction, yet your Teacher will not
hide him/herself anymore,
but your eyes shall see your Teacher. And when you
turn to the right or
when you turn to the left, your ears shall hear a word
behind you saying,
"This is the way, walk in it."*

– Isaiah 30: 30-21

# PREFACE

PLATO ONCE SAID, "An unexamined life is not worth living." Bending into our lives and learning how to read what is written there leads us to a consciousness that allows for change, integration, transformation, and wholeness. The root word for conversation is the same one for conversion. So, learning to read our interior realities and welcome what has marked our past selves can allow us to make choices that free up our gifts and heal our wounded histories. We may liberate what is deepest in us that longs to express who we are. That requires conversation; it requires contemplation, stillness, and a listening heart. My journals—which have extended over fifty years—have granted me that. My friendships have held me to that. Those who have accompanied me have held me in that, and slowly over the years I have matured and grown old.

In the following pages I will take you through my growing years, pulling poetry and prayer from various moments of my life. All is offering. Come, may you find traces of yourself here.

*Intricate patterns woven*
*Fine invisible threads*
*Bringing together moments of mystery*
*Learnings born of being Presence . . .*
*Of learning how to wait*
*Of being unhurried*
*While the Holy One ravels and unravels*
*The letting go's and the lettings in*
*Preparing the way for the final Abandonment.*
*The way of life*
*The way of Death*

*The way of Presence.*
*The way of always being with, in Sacred Mystery.*

*– October 14, 1993*

It has taken years for me to be able to hold the mystery of my creation long enough to let it reveal itself moment by moment, giving just enough information to inform my wakefulness for the time. Each of our lives begins specifically. Some of us are born into families that nurture and support us until we can be sent forth. Others come into life that carries more battering, less certainty; we are flung into finding our way with the hope of landing somewhere that allows us to know that who we are matters, and what we carry is meaningful for the world.

My mother was flung into the world carrying a child out of wedlock. That brought shame upon a family already bound by struggle. She was sixteen. Incredibly, she gave me two statements that I believed. The first is that I was born under a lucky star, and the second that I was conceived in love. I was six when she told me these things. When I was seven, my mother moved into a third relationship. Eventually, this one took us to a small city on Vancouver Island, where, as a ten-year-old, I was given my first real life choice. I was asked where I wanted to go to school. I chose to go to a school run by the Sisters of Charity of Halifax. I knew nothing about them. I wasn't a Catholic, but my stepfather was, and even though we weren't regular churchgoers, I was attracted to the mystery of these robed women.

In Grade 5, the one full year that I was there, I heard the third thing that would teach me to hold onto the thread of life when I had little else. I heard—in the midst of learning about antonyms and synonyms—Sr. Grace Marie say that "each of you is created for a special purpose." I shot up in my desk and decided to find mine.

Later, when I was sixteen, my stepfather said to my mother, "Either she goes, or I go."

I went.

And so, in this writing I will unveil the learnings that have brought me to the great privilege of finding home in my deepest self, connected to a Sacred Presence that has held, protected, guided, and saved me. I have been gifted many people along the way, as well as challenges that, at times, I didn't know I would survive. But I learned that we are very well made and are given what we need for the journey. I come to you with an offering that my journey has taught me, the power and gift in following the inner way of life, which perhaps may bless you. There are no formulas, simply invitations.

# PART 1

—

# Taking the Journey

## Introduction

WE ARE BORN into the magnificent invitation to become who and what we are, a magnificence of reality, of life. We are born out of mystery to become a revelation of possibility that carries the spark and dream of the first bursting of that sacred flare, when out of nothing the movement into the possible began. That is the big work of receiving the gift of our lives, opening up the deepest desire and longing that is invisibly written there, for the purpose of putting something of goodness in creation.

Some years ago, while in Toronto, I watched Tibetan monks making a mandala out of coloured sand on one of the floors in a shopping mall. It would take two weeks to complete. This work for them is as icons are for me. They used sand to create a sacred image. For these monks the mandala was holy work. For them each grain of sand used carried the energy of the divine. Sometimes they would take handfuls of sand to work with, and sometimes arrange the sand, grain by grain, in small areas. To write (paint) an icon, I prepare the wood, the image, the paint and bit by bit the image emerges. It is part of the prayer of the Byzantine tradition. It is a sacred work that requires presence, attentiveness, time, and a level of abandonment to follow the process. For me that is the way of our lives; sometimes things flow, and the path is clear. Other times only one grain of sand is worked with at a time. Sometimes the outcome is known and actualized, while other times we find ourselves in a desert, a swamp, or a surprising pocket of love. What is important is to step into life consciously and follow it, learn within it, respond to it, and allow it to be fashioned.

# CHAPTER 1:
## Holy Invitation - Graced Response

*A moment of Grace in time*
*A potter's hand moulding infinity as one*
*Moment upon moment*
*And mystery again*
*Breathless, fearless, and whole.*

ONE OF THE deeply graced moments in my life—and there have truly been many of them—was when I, at age forty, got to be part of a family that had triplets. Their biological aunt Joan and I would support the family in various ways. When the children were very little, we attended doctor's appointments. Where possible, we'd give

Mom and Dad a break by taking on childcare one day a week, a weekend in a month, or for a week in the summer.

On one occasion, when Joan and I were visiting the family, I was holding one of the girls giving her, her bottle. She was gazing at me in the way children do, with this great depth of seeing and somehow knowing, uncluttered in letting herself be seen.

Children, in their gaze, take us into themselves, do a walk-about, and decide if we can stay or not. For me, this is a profound moment in the relationship: it carries a deep call for reverence because the place I have been given entrance to is holy ground. This place of holy ground is the place of our original selves. It is the place of innocence, purity, and obedience to the Holy, to the Sacred. It is the place of sheer goodness, our best love. It's the place in us that is amazed by moments of holy synchronicity, filled with wonder at the beauty of a sunset, or the exquisiteness of an iris captured in a photograph. It is the place where, in sacred moments of love or unexpected kindness, we weep.

Out of this place, we fill with gratitude and joy and touch the dancing resonance of the universe that surrounds us with the sense of eternal presence and the knowing we will never die. These deep moments of meeting, simply given, invite us to awareness, to wakefulness to receive who and what we are in our humanity so that as we grow up, we avail ourselves of the wisdom that forms and fashions itself around this inner place, and we can bring to fruition the purpose of our existence, our creation.

For some of us, as we age, it becomes somewhat hidden and for some, it becomes close to being lost. Part of our journey is to unearth this original self, this place of holy knowing, of mystery and holy innocence, this God-image—for it carries our deepest freedom.

But to unearth this sacred, uncreated reality, we often need to do an excavation, remove debris, faulty beliefs, and defense mechanisms. It is big work, this journey inward. We must make way for grace and blessings for the whole of creation to come through our small, indispensable creation. And so, it is our task to become fully who we are, for in that wholeness lies our salvation, in that wholeness is our co-operation with the continued emergence of Sacred Presence, the breath of the universe unfolding as self-revelation.

# CHAPTER 2:
# Pilgrimage of Relationship

*I came*
*And light opened*
*Like stars beyond the gray*
*Being sent*
*on another pilgrimage*
*My yes is full*
*My heart is ready.*
*Bloom tree of life in me . . .*
*Bloom.*

*– July 1996*

I'VE BEEN ON this pilgrimage now for eighty years. For years this book has waited to take form, but all of my writing has gone into retreats, teaching, letters, and journaling. So how to unfold the essential elements I have been given, that have led me on this journey toward wholeness and integration? When I started out on my own some years ago, I could not have known I would be where I am today. My imagination could not extend this far. I have lived so much, made so many choices, developed so many relationships that have shaped me. In my young, wounded life, I could not have known that healing was possible, that dreams could actually be given birth, or the privilege of so much blessing in simply living in and following grace. And the secret to it all is knowing that all of life is relationship. All life requires our faithfulness, to show up to whatever the offering is, to bring of ourselves what we can, what we are meant to bring to each moment. I have learned that it is actually the responses to life's offerings that have essentially fashioned me, marked me, and eventually taught me. But I had to open myself to the invitation again and again.

I can say that as a very young child, I was very perceptive and observant, but like most young children I wasn't always a great interpreter. If my mother was sad, or if my mother and stepfather had a disagreement, I would see what was happening and wouldn't know if there was something I should do, or if it had anything to do with me. Sometimes things felt like my fault, but no one let me know that it wasn't. It was a time too when I formed some of my self-expectations. I remember my mother wanting me to learn how to embroider. She was wonderful at that art. But I couldn't really do it well when I was a five-year-old, and she got frustrated with me. I decided that I had to get things right the first time or I would lose her love, I would be a disappointment. There were many conclusions I came to about life, about situations which may have been true or not; somethings may have been my fault or not. Much of what I learned to believe about myself, and about my mother, about life, began in those early years. The experiences of acceptance, rejection, being loved or not, how to be in the world marked me.

I would say that for so many of us, that's how it is with life. Being wounded or hurt is part of the journey. What wounds or hurts us, breaks into, or covers that sacred place of innocence that we come into life with, and it happens mostly accidentally, unintentionally, even though there are those times when some hurts occur through lack of care, or abuse, or by intention.

My early perceptions and decisions followed me for a long time, until I developed the capacity to read my inner reactions, responses, and interpretations. I learned to distinguish between what was true of me and what were the faulty beliefs that wrapped themselves around my inner wounding and formed my defence mechanisms. There were so many self-beliefs that ran ahead of me in situations, events, and relationships. These would often show themselves in efforts to try and compensate for what I didn't have. And I learned that compensation only goes so far before the self-doubt and self-rejection returns.

So, the journey: embracing this inner unveiling of the seed-life-of-sacredness that desires to break into the gift of creation that you and I are, the weaving and unravelling, the listening and responding, the being held into the future with all the offerings of the Sacred Dreamer. That is my hope for you as you read these humble gatherings of my learnings and offerings of hope.

# CHAPTER 3:
# Wrapping My Life Around
# the Holy Thread

*My soul glorifies my God,*
*My spirit rejoices in God who is my Saviour!*
*For the God of Abundance has blessed me lavishly*
*and makes my heart and my body ready to respond.*
*The Greatness of God shatters the smallness of my world*
*and allows my littleness to have room to be received and sanctified.*
*This God of Creativity picks up my plans and shatters my illusions*
*and opens into life the dreams of my heart*
*beyond my greatest imaginings.*
*God packs each moment with Grace*
*so that I am not bound by my limiting beliefs,*

*and can become free to grow and to become fully who I am.*
*Tenderly, God empowers me to risk,*
*rooted in the Sacred,*
*God marks my path and allows godliness to be born out of my*
*own simplicity and humility.*
*God has named me servant and friend,*
*and out of that has called me to release the Reign of Sacredness.*
*Great is this God from Eternity to all Eternity world without end.*
*Amen*

*– March 4, 1999*

I HAVE LIVED as a part-time hermit for well into fifty years. In the beginning, it was not my conscious decision to live a life of celibacy and contemplation. It began to fashion itself in me very early in my life, and it began with the statement about all people being created for a very special purpose. There were wonderful men in my life, for whom I will always be grateful. They affirmed me as a woman, helped me know that I was loveable, took me home to meet their families—yet with all of what was offered as possibility for relationship and belonging, that deep thread of life that carried promise for the unfashioned dream, the dream of the possible within the context of marriage, was never awakened. Finally, one day in my mid to late twenties, I was in my car, at a stop sign, and I heard in me that I had to choose once and for all.

The wonderful man in my life at that time needed to be free to find someone else, because my intention in my relationship to him was not marriage but friendship, companionship, exploring universal truths. I realized I needed to find another way to live my relationships with men so that my unavailability to commitment beyond friendship was clear. I had to be clear in myself. I had to know what that looked and felt like, so that I didn't give any impressions of romantic interest. All this led to deep conversations and important relationships. And in 1970, it allowed me to choose the interior monastic path, the way of celibacy, contemplation and prayer as an alternative way of living in the world that has resonated and fashioned itself in me over these many years. My monastery was the world, my lifestyle was that of a Poustinik, that is one who goes into solitude praying for others and for the world.

The years of bumpy, imperfect growing deepened. I was always leaning into and following the inner life thread that would eventually become a path, a furrow, a way of being. I must admit that saying yes to becoming fully human is messy work. As challenging as some of it has been, I am grateful for it all. By nature, I tend to be an intense person. I have always taken life seriously since my beginnings. For a time in my life, I also took myself too seriously, till I learned this form of sensitivity, this self-interpretation, didn't free me for relationships. Instead, it turned my sensitivity against me, and this intensity, this sensitivity, needed to be fashioned, read, emptied, to serve life, to serve listening, and hearing, and healing. I needed to gather the fragments of my wounded self, gather the courage and strength of my heart and spirit, and follow the thread of life until I believed that the love that was deposited at the heart of my being was also for me.

But how does that become possible? In my early teens I was encouraged to consider marriage. My stepfather's mother found someone she thought would be perfect for me even though he was twice my age. But I felt I had to go back to school. I believed education could somehow "save me," would take me out of poverty and give me a chance to have what I never had. When I was fifteen, I got a job working at a bakery. It was great until the owners discovered I was underage and fired me. However, I found another job locally in the Keremeos hotel café, worked, and began to save for going back to school, and hopefully university. At the same time, I was still a significant helper at home where there were four small children and my mother, who often felt overwhelmed.

One early morning when I opened the café, a customer asked for oatmeal. I happened to cook it perfectly, and he said he owned a hotel in Osoyoos, and if I ever wanted a job, he would be glad to have me on staff. I really wanted to find a way to leave home and maybe find my way to Alberta where maybe I could live with an aunt and go back to school. All wishful thinking. I was only in Osoyoos for a couple of weeks, when my mother, with the help of a friend with a car, drove to Osoyoos, picked me up, brought me back, took me to a local RCMP office, and told the officer of my "disobedience." He, in turn, told me to obey my mother. I made no defence in front of this man, as angry and hurt as I was, I didn't want to diminish my mother—nor did I know what to say. It was decided, however, that I would return to school in Keremeos.

I had never attended school in this small town, and in the city where we had previously lived I'd barely finished Grade 8, as I had spent most of it caring for my mother and my half-siblings at home. However, near the end of that school year, as we were preparing to move as a family, my teacher, a Sister of St. Anne, told me that she believed that I could handle Grade 9, and she passed me on trial. I started the school year in Keremeos, found work after school, and helped at home as much as I could, until that fateful day of "either she goes or I go," when I moved back to Nanaimo, where we had previously lived as a family. I found a place to live, got a job, and went to school. Needless to say, it was challenging. I began sleeping through my classes. The school counsellor suggested that I apply to enroll in a one-year nursing course at the vocational school. There was one being offered for the first time. Problem was, I needed Grade 10. I met with the selection committee, knowing my chances were a bit slim, and amazingly, the board chair remembered me as the thirteen-year-old that had beaten the pavement to raise money for Hungarian refugees. Her good word brought me acceptance.

So I went into training, worked evenings in a restaurant, sang on a local radio show, went dancing Saturday nights, and began again to build a life. There were some difficult moments in that year. Sometimes depression and the feeling of being abandoned lurked in the shadows and edges of my mind, coming close to holding me hostage. But the thread of life was stronger and held me in the flow of life. There was one evening when I went with one of the band members to a party. When I went in the door, everything in me stood up in fear. It looked like an orgy, too much booze and drugs. I asked the man who'd brought me to take me home. I knew I could be destroyed there.

But the year held incredible moments of grace too. I invited my nursing instructress, a nurse from England, who knew few people in Nanaimo, to come to a Saturday dance with me. She met her husband there. One of the nurses at the hospital where I was training used to invite me to dinner to her place on Sundays when she was off. She served me roasted chicken with oven potatoes, and salad. She was newly from Ireland. Once I graduated, I never saw her again, until fifty-seven years later when I met her again at a Holy Week retreat at Bethlehem Centre in Nanaimo. She appeared one evening for one of the celebrations open to the public. I was able to offer her the gratitude that I carried in me from when I was seventeen. Her kindness marked me, and never left me.

Nursing was a great gift. It opened many doors for me to meet people, to continue to study, to eventually enter a religious congregation in Toronto, to leave and go on to Ottawa University. Through so many of these years I was introduced to philosophy, psychology, to different levels of suffering, to all kinds of goodness, and to the challenge of dreaming dreams of the possible.

My first job as a licensed practical nurse was in a little thirteen-bed hospital in Willingdon, Alberta run by Ukrainian Catholic nuns. When I first arrived to meet with the administrator to see if there were any openings for work, I sat in the entrance area. As I looked around, I noticed a picture of the Sacred Heart of Jesus above the entrance door. I felt a deep stirring in me and decided I had to work there. When I met with Sister Sylvia, a little nun about five-foot-nothing, she said they had no openings. I told her because there was a class of us that had just graduated, there were no jobs available on Vancouver Island, so I'd ventured on to Alberta, to test my luck. Whatever our exchange, she said she would talk to the board and see what she could do. I phoned a few times during the short time I stayed in Alberta with an uncle and aunt. After a couple of weeks, I was hired. I was hired, and I loved it.

Working with and for the Sisters brought my soul-self very much to the surface. I worked hard and found myself given all kinds of learning experiences. It was wonderful. I have one particular memory from a night shift. I brought my guitar into the operating room and sang some of my music to one of the young Sisters. I really did want to impress the Sisters with my goodness, wanted them to see me and appreciate me. They were kind to me.

Because I had been born in a town some short miles from Willingdon, and because I was renting a small room not far from the hospital, people were familiar with my mother's family, and my birth. I may have been eighteen, but stories live long in small communities. The women were curious and asked me a lot of questions that I didn't really know how to answer. I felt that I was being held against the memory of history and being judged as my mother might have been as a teenager. At one of the feather bees, where women from the community gathered to prepare feathers for making feather quilts, Sister Sylvia said, "Leave the girl alone." They put their curiosity in their pockets. I was grateful, even though I felt shame in being there. Shame clung to me often through my life; it took years of living to confront its power to diminish and prevent the emergence of specific aspects of my life. I'll save its teaching for later.

Another particular moment I will include from my time in Willingdon is a celebration I was taken to by a fine young man from the area. Ukrainians love music and love to dance—at least I did. My mother had taught me to dance when I could barely walk. She spent so many months on our little farm on her own that I was her main dance partner. At this celebration, there was wonderful music, polkas, waltzes, etcetera. Later that evening, this young man I was dating, and with whom I had shared my beginnings, including my father's name, asked me if I recognized one man I had danced with earlier in the evening, or if I had felt anything when dancing with him. I said no, and he informed me that I had danced with my father! I tried to remember him but couldn't. Nor did I have any idea if he knew who I was. I just assumed he asked me to dance because I was young and a good dancer. I know I wouldn't have pursued a conversation with him either, because I wouldn't have known where it would lead and my life at that time was challenging enough.

Because I had no cooking facilities, I ate my meals at the hospital. The staff room was about the size of a closet. Each morning as I ate breakfast, the sisters chanted morning prayer. As they prayed, I wept, for I heard something of my own soul awaken, something deep and longing in me that would eventually find expression. I lived and worked there about six months before moving on to Edmonton so that I could attend Alberta College to get more courses that would qualify me to attend university. I didn't finish that semester because, after finishing an evening shift at the Royal Alexandra Hospital, I was attacked and beaten, and would have been raped had the neighbour not heard my scream and scared off the attacker. When I returned to class the next day, black-eyed, the snide comments and judgements of my classmates re-victimized me. So, I didn't return to the college, just continued working.

From Edmonton, I moved to Leduc. I worked at the hospital and lived in a converted garage. Then I took time off of work to finish another semester of school. I turned twenty-one. That year I read Dostoyevsky's *The Brothers Karamazov*. His writing confronted my moral ethics, my compassion, or lack thereof. I began to journal that year.

That semester I lived on cornflakes and eggs brought to me by a local egg man. And I managed to have enough money to buy one book a month. I never did graduate from high school, but I got enough required courses to go to university. I share all of this to give you context, the beginnings of my essential formation, to explain how I was able to wrap my life around that sacred bond emerging in me, by clinging to the sacred life thread. This is how I was led to serve life in as much fullness as I could, through each stage of my life.

*Motivated by love*
*Moved by silence*
*I listen to the contractions within*
*my soul toward birthing.*
*Birthing the age-old process of bringing new life into*
*an already existing reality.*
*The old refined by time*
*softening and preparing*
*To welcome what is*
*not yet read . . .*

*– March 21, 1994*

# CHAPTER 4:
# Dreams of the Dreamer God

I believe that God dreams us, offers us the future
by running toward us.

*God of my heart*
*You hold me with joy in your creation.*
*God of my will*
*Melt me into simplicity.*
*God of my joy*
*Unfold me in wonder.*
*And in stillness*
*Hold me firm.*

I HAVE COME to know and understand something of Sacred Mystery as the Dreamer God. That holy reality that moved and danced above the waters dreaming of the possible before anything lived. In Jewish holy scriptures, she is known as Wisdom Sophia, or the Shekinah. She avails Herself to us in every breath, in every moment of joy, in every tear of grief and suffering, and lingers, rests in availability, desiring to guide us in the way of Truth. That's what she did in and with Jesus, fashioned him, instructed him in all ways and in all things. That's why by some, Jesus is called the Child of Wisdom.

Today theology and quantum physics inform each other in the mystery of emerging life and holiness, inviting us to take seriously the relationship of all life, of all things. We are invited to become conscious of being fashioned from the sacred dreaming and knowing of holy awareness, of holy consciousness.

In her book *The Path of Blessing*, Rabbi Marcia Prager writes:

> God 'speaks' and 'expresses' or 'presses out' God's SELF. From deep within the Infinite-Core-of Being, wave after wave of energy pours forth, expressing God's Self, and from deep within God all the letter energies of creation flow into the world. Material existence is born and evolves, drawn toward exceptional possibility: that Creation, emanating from the One Conscious Light, may itself achieve consciousness. (Then she quotes Genesis) "Then God formed the human form from the dusty earth. And breathed into it "Living Soul/Breath", and it became a conscious life (Genesis 2:7).[1]

Let me take you to one of my favourite passages on Sophia Wisdom, that I return to again and again, and with whom I spend time:

---

1    Prager, Marcia Rabbi. *The Path of Blessings*: Experiencing the Energy and Abundance of the Divine. First Jewish Lights Quality Paperback Edition (Woodstock VT. Jewish Lights Publishing 2003), p. 22.

*There is in her a spirit that is intelligent, holy,*
*unique, manifold, subtle,*
*mobile, clear, unpolluted,*
*distinct, invulnerable, loving the good, keen,*
*irresistible,[23] beneficent, humane,*
*steadfast, sure, free from anxiety,*
*all-powerful, overseeing all,*
*and penetrating through all spirits*
*that are intelligent, pure, and altogether subtle.*
*[24] For wisdom is more mobile than any motion;*
*because of her pureness she pervades and penetrates all things.*
*[25] For she is a breath of the power of God,*
*and a pure emanation of the glory of the Almighty;*
*therefore nothing defiled gains entrance into her.*
*[26] For she is a reflection of eternal light,*
*a spotless mirror of the working of God,*
*and an image of God's goodness.*
*[27] Although she is but one, she can do all things,*
*and while remaining in herself, she renews all things;*
*in every generation she passes into holy souls*
*and makes them friends of God, and prophets.*

– Wisdom 7:22-27

In my early exposure to religious thought, I was taught that before all was, God is. God is a reality that is uncreated. It's like God was all Spirit. I have since come to understand that on its own, Spirit can do nothing. She needs matter, soul, relationship to bring life into being. This point of entry that we are all invited to is the Christ reality. It names us as worthy, as loved, as invited to wholeness and oneness, as purposeful for the continued emergence of bringing to fruition the unveiling of Love. Love is the heartbeat of the Universe, attracting, fashioning, expressing, inviting creative response.

This holy mystery, this grace of self-revelation of goodness and love, that runs toward us from the future, it is this reality that pulsates at the heart of the essential life thread that I have carried that vibrates with "You are created for a special purpose." It says: "Be attentive, be awake, let it lead you."

> *Dreams of the Dreamer God . . .*
> *That we come to know and understand*
> *the gift of Sacred Presence.*
> *That we live and move in Grace.*
> *That we are infused with Sacred Presence.*
>
> *– June 2018*

# CHAPTER 5:
## Unveiling the Inner Dreamer

The Veiled Virgin[2]

HOW IS IT to be led? How is the unveiling of the dreams of the inner dreamer, the nudging, whispering, sometimes screaming desire of the soul activated? It is learning to read the realities and consequences of the choices made, the relationships lived, the deep moments of grace that attract, the deep moments of pain that sometimes feel like the edge of dying, those profound moments of loving that change, challenge, and transform what is.

---

2    Sculpted by Giovanni Strazza. Carved in Rome somewhere in the early 1850s. Housed in Presentation Convent Museum in St. John's N.L Canada.

Learning to read, to break open what moves within as feelings or sensations, learning to pause, to listen and to respond to the invitations of life day by day, because the essential learning, is that all of life is relationship. *All* of life is relationship! Every response to these offerings of life *is* what fashions, forms, and eventually challenges the willingness to become fully who we are, at the service of life.

We carry dreams in us. They begin early through our imagination. Our essential action, the composite of our capacity to bring something of the emergence within creation to fullness through us, teases in us to dream. In my very early years, I wanted to be a singer, to be famous, and when I was in nursing training, I sang every week on radio. Someone heard me and invited me to lunch and offered me an opportunity for a music career. Not until I'd finished my training, I said, so that if it didn't work, I had something to fall back on. I let that opportunity pass. However, throughout my life, I did sing. I wrote music, recorded, gave concerts for fundraisers to build schools, hospitals. I also thought of going into medicine, but I didn't think I was capable enough to succeed.

I wanted to be a nun, because I wanted to someday serve the poor in South America, but I was afraid I would somehow be too confined. I also entered because I wanted a place to belong, for my orphaned self to know home. I kept dreaming, processing my inner dreamer, following, journaling, so as to eventually fall into the crevice, the furrow, that responded to my inner sense of being. I essentially became a listener of life, a learner in process, a believer in the possible for healing and wholeness, and a lover of the Sacred in the abundance of Presence and Love. However, opening all of this reality up required learning to love, not from the safety of distance that I had managed to create, but to liberate the love that lived in me and exercise it intentionally. It required healing the original wound I carried that named me despicable. It required receiving myself in my goodness and truth and freeing myself from all the clutter of defences and faulty learnings.

Let me break this open just a bit more. In my very young life, I sang because I loved to sing, and write music, read books and imagine being seen. In this imagining, in this dreaming, the core of my longing was to be seen. To be deeply seen. I was seen through my music but remained essentially hidden. My guitar opened many doors for me, as did my free spirit and joyfulness. But I remained hidden in the heart of me. My nursing called forth all kinds of my gifts and qualities.

I intuitively knew how to meet people in their need for care, how to ease their anxiety, when and how to offer care and support. It also sharpened my curiosity and attentiveness around what brought children back to hospital again and again, what helped people recover, what is the power of the body to heal itself while cooperating with medicine. And what role does kindness and prayer play in this process?

What contributed to my inner dreamer the most were the people who came into my life as gift. So, so many people, Sisters, families, friends who loved me, were the greatest callers forth of my inner gifts and dreams of the possible. Let me close this section by saying that I am indeed the sum total of all of my relationships, relationships with people, with all of creation, with my deepest awareness of Sacred Presence that has held me and empowered me to live more fully than I had ever thought possible.

But it was not only to be seen; it was also to be believed, to be heard, to be understood, to be known. When we come to understand the "virginal" life, that is the uncluttered life that is better known as wholeness, that is the process, to move from not being known to being known to being one with self. This is the journey of healing, of excavating those faulty beliefs that imprison us, that prevent us from showing up to exercise our gifts, to stand firmly in ourselves.

## *Unveiling the dreams of the inner dreamer*

In my young life it wasn't unusual for me to hear that I was too free-spirited. One day someone would have to tame my passion for life, because I wasn't very conventional. I laughed too loud, I sang with gusto, I loved to dance. And I couldn't easily be contained. When I was around nineteen, a wonderful family offered me a home. I went there for a time. Because I didn't have a conventional method of studying, they thought they would help me by setting up a schedule so that I would do my classwork at a certain time, go to bed at a certain time. And for all their care, and generosity, it was all too confining and everything in me began busting out at the seams. So I left and found a two-room converted garage. But more on that later. For now, let me offer something that may appear as a contradiction, or maybe a paradox. I kept running into the face of God.

And the question that carried me was:

For what have I been created? To whom am I being sent? What is this dream, this longing, that moves in me, pushing at the interior walls of my heart, my spirit, to unveil and leave as blessing by my very life? Yes! Indeed! You have been created for a special purpose!

*What kind of God are you?*
*That haunts my wakefulness*
*Clinging to my spirit*
*Not letting me go to fate—*
*That form of conventional wisdom*
*Rationalizing outcomes because all that can be seen*
*Is what is on the surface of things to be judged*
*As our destination.*
*Of course, you have no choice but to cling to my spirit*
*Since it is out of Yours that I was formed.*
*Continue please to cling to me*
*Until I am awake enough to cling to you*
*And we move as one consciousness—*
*Full of response to your dreaming.*

*– January 2019*

In some ways I have always been a contemplative. But I hadn't named that reality in me as hermit. It wasn't until years later, when I welcomed someone to live in my home for a week at a time for spiritual accompaniment and therapy, that I was named Byzantine hermit.

Years before, I'd met and claimed my inner hermit while finishing up the necessary courses to consider university. I lived, for a time, in a residence for young women in Edmonton. It was a good place for me. My meals were prepared for me, I had companions to sing with and enter into great conversations with and share my day with, and I worked as an LPN nursing at the Royal Alexandra Hospital.

One day, while helping make a bed at the residence to welcome a new resident, one of the Sisters of Service asked if I had ever thought of becoming a Sister. True, I loved God; the thought had crossed my mind on occasion, but I hadn't given religious life real serious thought, my main focus was getting an education. I felt my life depended on it. However, the question awakened a deep reality in me, stirrings begun as a fourth and fifth grader, at this point, I seriously began to grapple with and follow. The Sisters were lovely; they sent me off to Toronto with a trunk, and what I might need when I got there. It was a wonderful moment of grace in my life. I thought perhaps I would eventually be a missionary, go off to Peru or Chile, somewhere that would allow for the unleashing of my passion for life.

In the year and a few months that I was there, I exercised all kinds of gifts. I helped people learn to drive, I was the bread maker, I used my skill as a nurse, I refinished furniture, I wrote music, I occasionally helped with prison ministry, and whatever else allowed me to be useful and creative. There was a young Sister there who introduced me to theology and gave me a window into Jesus. This human being, this Jesus, through his life revealed the potential of every human being to be a presence of love. That was the greatest gift in my time with these wonderful women. But not all of me landed there. Eventually, I came to realize that I was there for the wrong reasons. I did desire to follow God; I carried a deep knowing of belonging to this Source, this unnameable reality called God, but I deeply needed a place to belong, to know a sense of family and home, and that wasn't what was meant to be central in this calling to religious life.

For all the encouragement and affirmation I received, I always kept a place in myself distant. I carried something in me that felt that

I would not be able to actualize what dreamed itself deep in me, that in a religious community, I would have to conform to something that didn't fit me. Yet I would eventually make private vows, live my life committed to the unveiling of the dream of God through the gospels, solitude, prayer, and communal relationships. Not a simple, straightforward undertaking. But this path did allow for my big, wild spirit that did not squeeze into confined spaces easily.

When I was leaving the community, the Sister in charge said to me, "The door swings both ways, and if you feel drawn to return, we will welcome you."

Many years later, when I wondered if I was really being as faithful and vigilant as I could in front of another fork in the road, a friend said to me, "In all the years I have known you, everything you do is God-filtered, so you will do exactly what you are meant to do." I felt humbled and grateful. It is a real gift and privilege to be known and sent forth from this reality of community. And I find sometimes, when at the edge of change, it is tempting to try to recreate what was always known, that which felt safe, to avoid being stretched into the new. But the future always opens the possibility of something new, inviting a response so that nothing of life is lost. It is the grace of living in the creative process of being, becoming oneself honed into fullness.

# CHAPTER 6:
# Developing Inner Reading

I LIKE TO talk about inner reading: looking at our reactions, awakenings to situations, people who respond in ways that affect us in some way, conclusions that we draw in and through something said or not, what we interpret from a look or body stances. We are always reading what is in front of us more or less well. So, it is important to read what is written in those reactions, responses, or interpretations so that we can root ourselves both in what is true and see the reality that is before us, drawing us and pulling us into relationship. This involves clarifying our perceptions and conclusions. Our inner freedom relies on clear seeing, trusting our inner knowing, and being grounded in what holds us deeply in life. I often encourage people to know what they know and trust what they know. These are realities that reside in an inner depth, tested by life that reflects a truth of life, not opinion. This involves certain levels of excavation, disciplining and educating the ego to understand reality from a deeper level and not just move or make decisions out of reactions.

The interesting thing is that when we learn to live from this deep inner place of knowing, when we are willing to spend time moving around in it and trusting the wisdom that emerges from there, we rarely make poor decisions.

## *Examining Disappointments*

One pathway to inner knowing is examining our disappointments. What happens in me when I am disappointed? How do I examine the expectation hidden there, or the hurt that awakens, and perhaps the anger that comes with it? What did I hope for? And what need did it touch in me? I like to talk about real needs that come from unmet needs in our early lives, and those that come from "faulty" needs that we try to meet through some form of compensation.

For example, in my early life, I would live from my generous abundant spirit. I would pour myself into doing good things for someone, and hear their gratitude, but the resonance would not remain with me. So, I would seek out affirmation again. The affirmation landed in what I later named as a hole in my heart, like carrying a leaky bucket that couldn't hold what was given. I had to learn to ask: "Is what I did really a good thing? Is it true?" And then, if so, hold it in the truth of who I am in my generosity.

We develop various levels of sensitivity. If we are sensitive to criticism, then it becomes a filter through which we interpret reality. If we don't process it, we make it about who we are and so move into our defenses and fight, resist, and try to prove ourselves right—the other wrong. It becomes about our being rather than behaviour we can examine and learn from. I have a little formula that I like to use when I am working through things. "This is what happened. This is what I did, how I responded, what I felt. This was my intention, my hope, and finally, this is the learning." When I work with this information, I see what I believed, decided, and then look to generate options, or ways of dealing with what I lived.

## *Examining Our Original Wounds*

I spoke earlier of carrying an original belief that I was despicable. It was an essential part of me that became hidden deep in my inner heart. And it had a great influence on how I lived in relationships. I would name this as an Original Wound. Journaling, good friendships that carried what I would call deep conversations around becoming whole, exploring Spirit, working through misunderstandings, led me to free the imprisoned life held in the faulty belief I formed in this original wound of rejection that came at me through no fault of my own, or my mother's. It was a circumstance of life. With the help of a loving community, I learned to have this part of me exposed and received. I learned that in order for this place in me to heal, I had to dare to allow myself to be held in someone else's love and dare to open my inner eyes in front of it, to allow it to enter my own heart, and I had to receive it. In that very significant moment, I let go of the lie that kept me hidden, the lie of being despicable. Life carries pain, suffering, and a great desire for wholeness. Three things I never lost in the face of suffering: courage, gratitude, and wonder. Those were gifts from my mother.

Most of us carry a sacred wound, an original wound that forms some of our belief system about ourselves, others, and the world, and even the universe. It generally interferes with our perception, our relationships, and tends to generalize what forms around it. It can be healed, and it can teach us, because it carries the knowledge of what is missing in the world. If we identify with it, it can pull us into a hole, drag us into depression. Something else that perpetuated this wound in me was not being believed; it was a reflex that lived long into adulthood, until finally I reached that place of freedom where I no longer needed to be heard, understood, or seen. I could receive affirmation and verify it with the truth I knew of myself. Sometimes it was only in bits and pieces, but the practice of checking to see if what I'd heard was true helped me to claim myself in my humanity.

So ultimately, it was not so much to do with not being in relationship but standing well in myself, allowing me to not have to prove who I am nor to expect people to be for me what I was meant to be for myself, or to give me what I already had or knew of myself. This is not being self-reliant, not being independent, but interdependent. The wisdom of the sacred wound is inviting us to put in place in the world, the universe, what is essential for life, that which cannot be known until our work allows it to be given to life's emergence.

*So many faces of suffering,*
*so many realities that take us out of ourselves,*
*tempting us to hide from life,*
*the embrace, the journey.*
*What is it to suffer? To grapple with choices?*
*How to choose, what to choose?*
*How to penetrate mystery?*
*How to stay in the moment,*
*the now, and be found by God*
*when we are too weary to seek?*
*How to be held by mystery,*
*God's ever presence loving us beyond ourselves?*
*Suffering takes us out of control,*
*challenges our rigidity,*
*confronts our expectations,*
*our wants, and strips us*
*to look at what we need:*
*Essentials for freedom,*
*essentials for love.*
*Receive me O God in my littleness.*
*Receive me O Sacred and Holy Mystery*
*out of which I have come.*
*Be One in and with me that I may see,*
*know, feel your Presence*
*so that I may rest in you and know I am not alone.*

*– February 28, 2019*

# *Examining Our Defensiveness*

One of the beliefs I developed around my original wound was that "there was no one there for me," so I was on my own. So, I developed the mechanism of self-sufficiency as a defense. If I didn't need people, I wouldn't be rejected by others, nor would I be rejected by myself for not being enough. Certainly, this mechanism is isolating and can be a good foundation for self-pity. Defense mechanisms form to provide levels of protection until we can protect ourselves from within when we are able to stand on solid ground. Of course, it requires work to see and to listen into them, to understand their function and what they are protecting us from. That means working with our histories, coming to know our past selves. It means coming to know what we relied on to survive, exploring our attributes, our strengths. That is also why it is good to find the positive function of our defense system—because it carries strengths that can be used to build life, and not just keep it at bay.

Defense mechanisms are formed early in life as a way of protecting it. Anger, for example, is meant to be a defense of life, but instead it gets used for winning, for overpowering, and diminishing. Silence is sometimes used to punish, hiding the anger or rage that is woven into its fabric. It is important to work on whatever defense mechanisms we have built so that we can live authentically from our deep inner freedom that is rooted in our truth, our love, compassion, integrity, and an ethic that liberates life in us and around us.

One defense mechanism I used was the Grouch. When I was overtired, overworked, I resorted to the grouch that created space around me. When I lived with someone it kept them at bay, when I was alone with it, it allowed me to resent, blame, feel sorry for myself. And it was all my own doing. It was me not allowing my limits to be respected, being over-responsible and believing I had to "do it all." I carried the familial and cultural rule of "can't rest till all the work is done." If not fully available to the point of exhaustion, I was not a good, caring person or Christian. This is different from living love to its very limit, to the very end of it. We learn to know its boundaries. We are meant to live love to its fullness, but not to the point of burn-out.

We are meant to give our full measure, but not to the point where there's no life left to give. For me, one aspect of holiness is giving my all—no more and no less. Holiness is unveiled in the integration of wisdom and inner seeing that calls forth the gift and grace of life shared. This doesn't mean that I don't run out of steam or feel exhaustion. But it isn't the kind of fatigue that buries itself in my bones and sinews and bleeds me from loving in relationship. That kind of giving is ego driven, not love or life driven. That kind of exhaustion not only avails us to dis-ease, but to sickness. All that is to say that we need to bend into our reactions and read what is inside of them so that we can be free to address what needs to be addressed, free our lives from what sticks to us as expectations, unmet needs, hurts, anger, etcetera.

Overprotection damages as deeply as rejection. Children can then grow into adults who try to earn love by the refrain "try hard to try harder" to be loved, seen, cared for. Some people discover that their greatest strength is weakness, which can hold people hostage where others become trained to do for them what they are meant to do for themselves. This mechanism, this attitude, doesn't allow the care given to be received, to rest in the person. It is easy to cling to what is wounded in us. What we haven't been taught well is that we are very well made and have everything we need for our life journey. Part of our work is the healing journey, but that is only one aspect of it. The biggest invitation in our life journey is to become fully who we are, and in that emergence, we in turn contribute to the emergence of the world, the earth, and the universe. One of the other essentials for this is life-giving relationships, relationships that call us forth.

It takes a long time to free ourselves from our defense systems and distinguish them from self-protection. Our defense systems work at protecting us from harm. We develop them very young, and they are necessary so that we don't get destroyed. But we tend to hold onto them too long, well into our adult life, living them as if we are still too small, too little to care for our lives. We fight to be seen. We fight to be heard, to be understood, to be believed, to be accepted, to be significant, to be known as good.

As we heal and become more deeply rooted in our own solidity and strength, we learn how not to place ourselves in situations that are harmful, or violent or diminishing. We aren't "nice" people who somehow believe that being a victim makes us good and holy. Unnecessary suffering, faulty martyrdom, is not redemptive or holy. It takes a long time for us to work through and relinquish the supports of these belief systems. There are things that we can tolerate out of an acceptance of differences, irritants, differences of opinion— sometimes strongly—but we are not lessened by it even if we end up being wrong. But these things don't diminish us, they don't abuse us in our humanity. Now living in any form of community is a place of purification. It requires a willingness to be transformed, to be changed. It challenges us to run into our differences and learn to talk, to express ourselves, have disagreements, and see ourselves and the other. It means talking long enough so as to reach the other side into understanding, but not necessarily agreement. It means listening inside our own selves to find what we value, what we mean, what we can live with and what we cannot.

In my young days, I didn't know how to do that well. I didn't like to be wrong, criticized, judged, or put down. I didn't always understand why some people didn't like me, although I know some people considered me a bit wild or too much or having too much passion. And I learned to accept that about myself. I was "too much" sometimes, even over the top sometimes, and I did and continue to have a lot of passion for life, for people, for the Sacred and God, for the desire for wholeness, taking life seriously, for people to choose life and live it well, for justice and fairness and truth. Life has always been serious for me, and I learned to take it seriously and myself less so.

Over and over again I had to learn not to turn my sensitivity in on myself because it led to unnecessary suffering, guilt for not being enough, not doing enough. It was always much easier to admit when I made a mistake and learn from it or keep learning from it until I got it. I have never really been afraid of my failure; I have always had enough courage to embrace it. What had the capacity to undo me was shame. Shame would drive me out of relationships, out of cities; it would send me into hiding. And it worked itself in me even while I did so many wonderful things, lived so many meaningful relationships and realities. Shame was at the heart of my original wound, surrounding, encapsulating my original innocence that judged me as despicable. And I had to come to the point where I stopped believing it and stood up for myself. I had to evict the power of the lie that kept me in bondage. It was big work. This kind of work required my journals, good friends, community, and someone who could see deeply enough to accompany me, so that I could find myself on the other side of it.

## *Examining Our Self-Pity*

Self-pity is a cycle that digs a hole, allows for weeping but teaches nothing. When I lived it, it made me feel helpless to take charge of my life. Holding sorrow or sadness or feeling sorry for oneself can open up inner understanding for loss, for longing, for aloneness, that needs to find a way into self-care. Feeling sorrow for a moment in life, that is challenging, is not self-pity. It is grieving for what isn't, or what was, or what could be and isn't. It is that moment when I would have to work to find my way through and use that very significant prayer written by Reinhold Niebuhr: "God grant me the serenity to accept the things I cannot change, the courage to change the things I can, and the wisdom to know the difference." This prayer would "force" me to choose life, to work at it because the self-pity denied a positive outcome or sense of future.

Pity is not compassion. Pity is not sympathy. If I examine when and how I have lived pity in a situation, it is in those times where I have kept myself distant, disengaged, and it carried a form of judgement that said: "If they really wanted to, they could change their situation, but obviously they don't." And of course, there was the edge of arrogance that accompanied it: "I found a way through, so can they!" No mercy.

However, compassion is a different reality. It comes from the same root word that womb does. The Hebrew word for compassion and womb is *rekhem*.[3] Womb love allows for soft landings, for holding the other in respect and compassion. It allows for being open to story, for how the person landed in that situation, for what was known and what wasn't, for what was needed and for what was ignored, what choices were made, and what were missed. I have found that compassion allows me to hold the life of the other and be sad with them, and at the same time be powerless before their reality. When I have listened to people in deep pain, I knew I couldn't change things for them, but I could put myself under the suffering, the pain, and shoulder it with them, hold it with them, while they found their way through. Powerlessness did not, does not, mean being helpless. Compassion wraps the other in love; it is the willingness to relieve the suffering of another.

Compassion is a natural gift of our nature. It is connected to the Breath-of-God in us. It is important for us to understand how this gift of compassion lives in us, how it moves in us, so that we can exercise it, offer it from the depth of our deepest freedom and be a presence of Love. Keep in mind that compassion holds the reality of the other and seeks to relieve the suffering without making it our own. It carries patience, wisdom, and perseverance. Sympathy helps us understand what the other is feeling because it reflects and awakens something of our own experience. Empathy allows us to be in the presence of anguish, to be present and non-judgmental before it, without engaging in it. It is one of those times we say, I'm sorry this has happened to or for you, and we move on. Sympathy evokes a feeling of understanding because it is something we have experienced in some way. It's the "been there, done that" feeling. So, we can offer understanding and presence in the moment. It is what we often express at funerals. Sympathy and empathy are companions to

---

3    A good reference for this is Marcus J. Borg in his book Meeting Jesus Again for the First Time: The Historical Jesus & The Heart of Contemporary Faith. (New York, NY 10022 First HaperCollins Paperback Edition 1995) p. 48.

compassion. Each of these carry a disposition toward mercy and an availability to grace, giving direction for what is realistic and possible for the context: What is ours to do or to be.

One caution I have in relation to each of these attributes is to avoid being seized by the emotion and make the other's suffering or anguish our own, because when we do, we are no longer present to the other.

In my young life, I often grappled with how to be in front of what life offered in a day, what to choose, how to respond and how to live. I both trusted and didn't trust people. I avoided clingy, needy people. I had an allergy to them, even though I carried some of that reality in myself. Sometimes I got tired of leaning into having to find my inner strength and courage. But not having anyone to rely on, I had to choose myself or move into despair.

When I was in my late teens, living in one-room rentals—or the famous converted garage without plumbing, needing to go next door to use a bathroom or get water—I often felt sorry for myself. In those moments I lived anger toward my mother and stepfather; I felt alone and abandoned. There was one time when I remember I had no place to live, so I found a temporary place. The temporary place I stayed at was in a basement. I don't even remember when, where, or with whom that was. What I do remember is the darkness of the space and not having the energy to really stay with the struggle. I found getting up to face the day difficult, found myself crawling into an interior hole of depression. I wasn't there long because the woman who owned the house came down to the basement and told me I had to get up and get a life because I couldn't continue to stay there. I left, and I did. Self-pity was a luxury I couldn't afford if I wanted to finish courses for matriculation and get to university and find my way out of poverty.

The converted garage in Leduc carried blessing for me. I realized one day that my tomorrow depended on how I lived today. I said to myself that I could only be happy tomorrow if I found a way to be grateful today. And I managed each day to be grateful for the main staples of cornflakes, eggs, and coffee with the occasional can of

Prem, Spam, or canned meat. Fortunately, I learned to journal, to write for myself, to talk with myself, so that I could face myself and choose life again and again.

And there were also good people in my life who I could occasionally spend time with, or receive care from, be in relationship with, who believed in me beyond my own self-belief. I lived a paradox. While I had a lot of courage, and I believed that I could do and would live, I also didn't trust that relationships could hold me. We are complex beings. We can understand, know, and miss so much along the way. We have to grow into who we are, for some of us we have to choose to excavate who we are when caught or held in the rubble of our history. Being able to carry sorrow that doesn't imprison us can fashion compassion toward ourselves and others. It can fashion our inner vision to see what is missing in the world, empowering us to help fashion the missing pieces, because we have known it so deeply.

One of my realizations has been around saying "I'm sorry" over and over, and then not accepting forgiveness, perpetuating patterns of self-rejection, of perfection, of believing the lie that no matter what I do, it will not be enough. Recognizing this, looking at the motivation, breaking into what it carries so relationships can be lived, is part of the reclaiming of life and sharing the learnings. I will look at forgiveness more fully later.

There is a gospel story that carries the invitation to own our lives, deal with our histories that I would like to bend into. It is in John 5:1—18. It's the story of a person who was sick for thirty-eight years. This person complained they didn't have anyone to carry them down to the healing pool. Jesus came along on the Sabbath, a day when no one is to work or do anything and said to this person, "Take up your mat and walk." In other words, take hold of your life, walk, take hold of your history, and walk. In this gospel it is Jesus who says that. It could be a friend, a Spiritual Director, it could be a therapist who is this Jesus to us, or it could be our own inner courage that says, "I will accompany you, be with you, but you have to decide, you have to choose." That's how it is with loss and grief, with a wounded history.

It can swallow us up. We can sit and wait for the rescue boat to come and save us from ourselves. But choosing life is within us, we are given what we need to make those choices, to reach into life. And when we do, our task is to hold it tenderly in us, cry out, scream, weep, sleep, walk, stare into the darkness waiting for light, and then—we need to rise up so that the gift of life which was given by another, or held within our own being, is not lost to self-centredness. Self-centredness leads us to self-pity. Self-pity bleeds us of the future.

When we see another's goodness, then our love can call them to it. When we believe and see deeply enough, they can begin to see themselves through our eyes, our belief. But they have to believe in us, believe in our capacity to see and be before them, so we have to be attentive to polish our glasses in truth and compassion. We have to be aware of the authority we carry so that it is used for life and not for power, for unveiling the Grace given for each life movement and not for imposing our own will on the other. And so, it is for us, it is for me, to learn from Jesus, to love who and what God loves, to see as God sees, and to be as God is in the world in the fullness of our humanity.

And so, for me, it is to be the God-bearing One, named as the Theotokos in Byzantine theology. It is to find that interior place that is wordless, that place in me that washes my life with wisdom and knowing, that rests me and teaches me, awakens me to clarity and fidelity, gives me images that affirm and challenge me so that nothing that is given of life is lost. It is also in this place that people linger and speak to my heart.

## Process of Healing

There is a process to following in coming to name what wakes up in us.

1. This is what happened.
2. This is what I did, felt, understood.
3. Then this is what I did.
4. Then this is what happened.

5. What was touched, awakened in me?
6. What are my choices in front of this?
7. What can I say, do, ask, to find understanding within myself and within the relationship?
8. How can I own what belongs to me, my reactions, my beliefs?
9. What did I want in and through this reaction, interaction?
10. What had I hoped for?
11. And what would it look like once I had it?
12. What needs to happen, or what do I need to do, or understand for me to have what I want, need?

It is to follow the interaction because that is what being in relationship carries. Interactions for what builds, what challenges, and what tears down. Something I find helpful is an A, B, C exercise I learned somewhere years ago. That means step outside of the interaction. Watch myself and the other interact. Watch the facial expression, the voice tones, try to be in the other's shoes and then back in my own.

There is so much complex reality in trying to live our relationships well. There are so many pieces we need to continue to work at in ourselves that puzzle us, anger us, delight us, grateful-fill us, and invite us to explore so that our deepest freedom can be released.

Going through my journals, I noted that there were many times when I had found myself facing realities I didn't know what to do with. There were times in my young life when I would be in front of injustice and not know how to address it, or where to bring it so that someone else might know what to do. There were times when I didn't understand someone's intention and got caught up in my judgment, left the relationship and lived with regret for years. I didn't know how to talk about many things, how to let go when I was hurt or diminished, or how to hold my own with gentleness and truth. In my better moments I would step aside and wait so that I didn't trample on what was fragile and delicate. Other times I would push back because I didn't feel there was room for who I was. My go to was often to just drop out, give up and leave. But most of the time

I worked at myself, worked in the relationship because I knew and continue to know that what saves us is relationship and community.

We grow up through relationships, we find ourselves and are able to name ourselves through relationships with all the struggles, challenges, and blessings they carry. In going through my journals, I find myself deeply saddened sometimes for my inability to recognize, know, or see fragility hidden beneath a struggle. Other times I am deeply moved by the tenderness and love that so filled my heart and life. And generally, I am just grateful that I had and continue to have the opportunity to be called forth through community and friendships and my work of accompaniment. Perhaps what I know best in this time of my near-ancient years (I have a young friend who, when he was little, called growing old "becoming an antique") is that we walk this path but once.

So, it is important for me to be faithful in and through each moment of life's offering in front of me. Gratefully, I don't carry shame anymore. Gratefully, I stand in my goodness and grace without compromise. Gratefully, the God that I know and love, this big sacred reality, is enough for me so I can rest in the grace of the present, offer myself, and receive who and what is before me, and in this I co-operate in liberating the sacred from some outer realm and find this source and bigness in me, around me and in the depth of mystery beyond me. Always when we meet there is a place that moves between us. It is activated before we even speak. We fill it with imaginings and projections, so what do we walk into: What lives and moves between us even before we speak or are conscious?

Something else I notice as I gather my journal writings is how often I find that those with whom I am blessed to live have the gift of creating beauty. It is wonderful to be able to walk into a room and be faced with beauty. My young and early life was spent living in almost stark simplicity. I had little, so lived with a survival mentality of only the basics. It was always enough for me. My luxuries were books, fountain pens—not expensive ones, but good ones—and a camera. Eventually I moved up from a little brownie to a Nikon. Even now my way is simple, with great appreciation for beauty imagined by the creative imagination of others, and of course, my camera, which is a lens into a world of sacred imagination.

What I do have and carry though is an abundance of love. In the presence of the sacred, of goodness, of nature, of what is at the heart of people, I fill with love. It is a mystery to me how wonderfully made we are, how capable we are to become fully who and what we are even though it is costly. The cost is always letting go and letting God, letting go of our faulty learnings, letting go of our false sense of self built up by our egos. All of which we chose because it was the best we knew how to do; it was often the best others had to offer us. Yet it is in every generation that we must bend into life in us, bend into our history to unravel what is stored there and unveil the creative genius of our own souls. Our early learnings can be filled with self-rejection, self-doubt, fear of other's judgements, desire to be perfect, which can place us above others, with the false belief that if we try hard enough, we will be accepted not for who we are but for what we do, and the illusion of self-sufficiency.

Something I have had to work on in myself is my immediacy. I have had the tendency to respond immediately before thinking. I would drop things I was in the middle of to respond to something else, especially if it had to do with caring for something or someone. It has taken years to discipline that reality in me.

My own immediacy brings me to my godson when he was about two-and-a-half or three. I was pushing him on a swing and said we were going to have to stop soon, and he jumped off before I could get the swing stopped. In the 'soon', he obviously heard now. His immediacy frightened me because he could have been hurt. And it is that reality I had not lost. And unfortunately, immediacy caused me to postpone things I wanted to get done or had started and not finished and led me to inner frustration. The hazard in that is that I would eventually overload inside and withdraw.

I learned young to be what others wanted me to be. My job was to be available, to do and be for them. This was where I found my acceptance and place. I learned to believe there wasn't anything that I couldn't do, so I overdid, over tried, overworked, or over availed myself. Always at stake was my being seen as good, as strong, as capable and concerned about the danger of someone not having what they needed to live. This was an early learning.

Something I have also learned is that my body carries wisdom. It helps me know when I am anxious, in danger, how much wine I can drink, how much sugar I can take, how long I can visit so that I am not depleted, or when I am at the edge of a cold. Before certain realities that carry danger or oppression, I must be attentive because anxiety forms around my heart—literally three or more inches around. And I feel the tension in my solar plexus and deeper down into my entrails. I have learned that when I don't have enough meaning in my life, I can move toward a sense of depression, which I have come to understand as not exercising my creativity.

We need communities of love, not only to facilitate emergence and healing, but to dispel darkness and blindness. Self-reflection that leads to consciousness, relationships that facilitate integration and tolerance, patience that creates space for difference—all are part of the call for healing and wholeness through sacred wisdom.

# CHAPTER 7:
# Shame, Guilt, and Regret

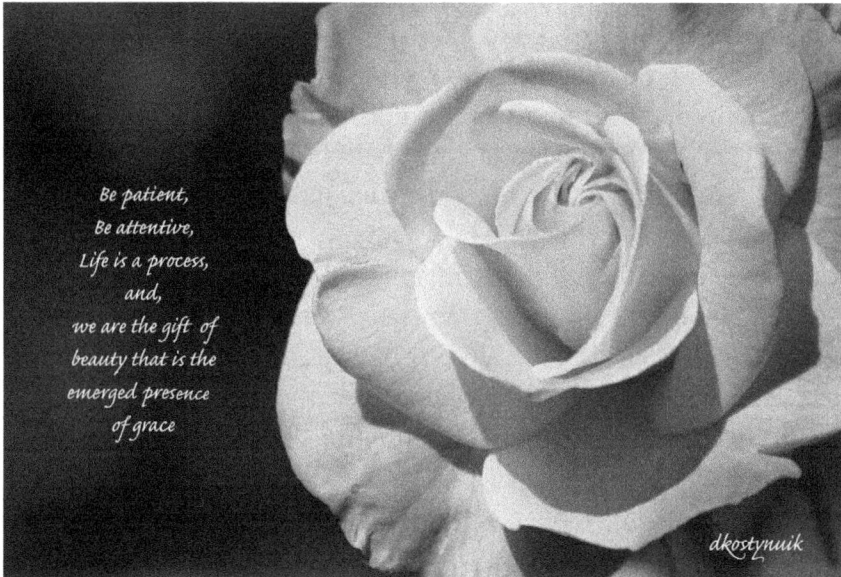

Be patient,
Be attentive,
Life is a process,
and,
we are the gift of
beauty that is the
emerged presence
of grace

dkostynuik

*Reality has a challenging face.*
*Honesty is fraying, sometimes desiring growth,*
*realness embraced by some kind of tender giving.*
*Arrogance is sharing your truth without loving.*
*Humility is seeing what is no more and no less.*
*It encourages truth and life to emerge.*

*– August 8, 1974*

IN LOOKING AT my life, I suppose one of the central elements that
I carry is regret. I regret so many aspects of my past, so many ways

that I have not lived relationships well, where I have simply dropped out when I felt I had done something wrong. I am not talking about guilt. What I've learned about guilt is that it boxes us in to build certain kinds of defenses. It tends to give us permission to never change, because we have come to believe that guilt is enough suffering in itself. What I've known in myself, and what I have seen in others, is that it doesn't teach us. I've seen people so paralyzed by guilt they can't find a way to choose life—as if the suffering of guilt was life itself.

Guilt leads to shame. I have known the shame of the woman bent, unable to look up, feeling undeserving of being held in the eyes of love. Shame requires forgiveness, guilt requires truth and honesty. Then regret can teach. I am talking about having been led by shame. Shame bends us over, disabling us from standing well in ourselves. It judges us as unworthy of good, of love, of relationships that call us forth to be more than what we imagine ourselves to be.

I remember one instance in my late twenties, perhaps early thirties, when I was visiting a family. We had a good relationship, enjoyed each other's company. I don't remember the conversation around the dinner table, but it was something to do with justice, perhaps even the church, and the place of women. Whatever it was about, I expressed great anger, not at anyone there, but toward an issue. I had not known that kind of anger since I was in Grade 6, when I went to a small country school, and every day I was hounded and bullied by a small group walking in the same direction as I was, going home. One day I'd had enough, and I took after them with my lunch kit. Fortunately they ran faster than me, or I might have hurt someone terribly. I frightened myself with my rage. I began to be watchful of it in myself, because I was afraid it could be too strong for me. It was a moment of learning. As a guest at a certain dinner, however, I watched myself escalate in anger. I even stood up to emphasize my point. I left there feeling my deep shame of perhaps having offended them, of having misrepresented myself, of needing to prove a point, and in the end not knowing what this family felt or thought. I never visited again.

This was another teachable moment. In the Catholic tradition we have what is known as the sacrament of reconciliation. Fortunately, I trusted the priest in the parish I was in, and could "confess" this sin, this missing of the mark. It was a space to entrust to another human being my inappropriateness and receive acceptance and forgiveness for this action. I have had many missing-the-marks in my life, and my way of coping was always to simply leave the relationship.

Shame is a powerful emotion. It holds us in a place of helplessness, where no matter what we do, it never makes up for what we did; we believe we are never enough. For me, in that place I carried the judgement of being despicable, and shame fed this belief.

Now, this reality of shame wasn't always active. There was more to me than that, but it was certainly a place that denied entry to love. It always held me at the edge of love so that I was an onlooker. Shame tended to be sticky and clung to a part of innocence in me that wouldn't allow me to forgive myself, even though I had "confessed" my sin.

So it was amazing to me when, many years later, I met the woman in whose home I had raged, and found that what she remembered of me was not my rage, but my sitting on the floor singing to and playing with her children. I had been a slave to the image of myself as a bad person. Self-hatred, self-oppression is seductive. It sucked me in when I was very young. No matter how much love surrounded me, when I misrepresented myself, shame was the lens through which I evaluated myself.

Regret, on the other hand, carries a point of learning, and when worked with, leads to conversion, which means a change of mind. This eventually leads to transformation, which then allows making decisions that facilitate life. It is helpful to note that the root word for conversion is the same as the one for conversation. In living relationships well, in working with regret, we need to have enough conversation. Having a journal has been a tool that brought so much clarity to my living well. It is a tool that helped me clarify what I have carried interiorly. It has deepened my relationships with myself, others, reality, and with Sacred Mystery. What also helped me was to have a spiritual accompanier. Sometimes that was a very good friend, and other times it was someone I chose, who could hear what was deepest and hidden in me.

To clarify further, shame is different from being embarrassed. We recover from being embarrassed, but shame roots itself near our innocence and is a judge that never tells us the truth about ourselves. The lie shame carries must be recognized, named, and its power evicted. A lie is never changed because it is always a lie. We learn to stop believing it. We disempower it and replace it with the truth. Humility is seeing and accepting ourselves how we are—no more and no less. Our essential journey is becoming fully who we are, reaching beyond our faulty beliefs and living from our deepest freedom where we meet our most authentic self, our best self.

There is a purpose to our creation. For me, that carries a mandate. In it, we are meant to bring to completion an aspect of creation that requires our faithfulness, our creativity, our emergence through our loving and relating, our many opportunities for learning through our shortcomings and missing of the mark. It isn't about being flawless or perfect. Life is too real for that. It is about authenticity. It's about knowing our goodness. It's about activating our inner courage to live life in such a way that we give it away and embolden it to serve what is empowering emergence and making whole.

## *One Last Reflection on Shame*

In 1987, I found myself carrying a deep weariness. Whenever it surfaced, I had no strength. Also, I found myself carrying a form of depression with the fatigue. I had the sense that if something didn't change, I would die within the next two years. When I was working or writing, this was not in my awareness and didn't interfere with the present. The depression was elusive. It would just show up with a sense of lifelessness. Something else I carried was withdrawal. It was almost imperceptible and would live near the place of my solitude. It's not the same thing. One is holy and full of sacredness, and the other a place of isolation. Over the years of love and healing, it had gotten smaller and only a root remained that needed to be dealt with. I began to use active imagery to work with it. Then in time I had to bring it to the group so that this small part hidden would be called out.

One incident of withdrawal began with a falling out with Joan. I don't remember what it was about, but it usually involved my feeling that she projected always being right and knowing better than me. Often, I could just let it be. We had lived community long enough that I could let it go. However, this day, I dropped into a place in myself that really personalized what felt like criticism or just not being enough. It was an old place in me that I wasn't finished dealing with. And so, I withdrew to my room and disappeared into myself. It wasn't that I moved into self-pity but that I moved into a deep pain in myself that I didn't have understanding around. Joan came into my room and found me lying on my bed, hands behind my head. She sat at the end of my bed, asked me how I was, I said I would work it out. In other words, leave me alone. She stayed. I spoke about my feeling of not measuring up, of never being enough. As we talked and the hurt in me began to surface, she suggested I speak with Jeanne, Claire and Raymond who were part of our life sharing group and who came when she called.

We sat in a circle together. I knew they were prepared to do whatever I needed for me to find my way through what was living in me. The symptoms I shared with them were the voicelessness, the helplessness, and the withdrawal. As I began to try to speak the trembling in my body began, and voiceless tears came, and I couldn't move. Finally, I fell to my knees and crawled to each one so that I could allow them to look at me and so that I could look back and receive their look of love. It took all my strength and will. When I came to Raymond, I wept as he simply looked at me from his deep graced compassion. Slowly, gradually, in a sacred silence soaked with love, I found enough voice to speak.

The deep work of reclaiming the very small part of me that didn't have permission to exist began. I found written there the shame of being born an infant instead of an adult. I found the lie that named me despicable. Body memories came. One was of being left in the crib, my mother prevented from coming to me sometime in the first couple months of my life. Another memory was of my grandfather preparing to kill me with a chair or a shotgun, my grandmother arriving just in time (I talked with my mother about this sometime later, and she confirmed the body memory).

Many times in my life, this hidden part had led me to both dependence and co-dependence in relationships. I would become infatuated with people and, in a sense, lose myself to them. Reclaiming this part of me was big work. I was grateful to the gift of community that saw me deeply enough to call this little part out. They showed me I didn't need to hide behind my strength to deal with it; I could be held by my own strength as I brought it forth. Fear of being seen came from the shame of needing, of being little. I had absorbed the shame of my mother and of the family. The truth is that God wanted me to be born. And I had to be born somewhere. Claiming my original littleness allows the woman that I am to be whole. Living shame hides who we are, judges who we are, disqualifies our existence.

# CHAPTER 8:
## Decisions

*What is it to pray if not to move and breathe in relationship to all*
*that is*
*Sacred, and good, and full of the desire for the holy.*
*Is not the Sacred in your breath,*
*in your body,*
*in all of creation that lives and breathes around you?*
*Are you not an expression of that which has birthed you,*
*formed you, invited you to the whole in which lives the Holy?*
*Are you not held in Creative Spirit,*
*that Holy Breath,*
*the breath in all that has come into being?*
*Rest then in breath, that prayer may rise in and out of you as Grace—*
*holding life, longing with life for the revelation of the One who Is.*
*Pray then that you may see as God sees, love as God loves, be as*
*God is*
*simple and holy.*

*– September 14, 2019*

OUR LIVES ARE a tapestry of decisions. Every decision carries some form of goal, desire, hope, or perceived need. Each decision carries perceptions of potential outcomes. Sometimes they are simple decisions, involving questions like, "How do I want to live my life this day, what do I want to give my life to, and what meaning will it have for my heart, my mind, my spirit, my relationships?" Or as simple as, "What will I choose to eat today? Will I choose to walk in the rain? Will I say "yes" to this phone call, or meet with this or that person?"

Choices made consciously or unconsciously give a direction for each moment. So again, it is the invitation to be awake, to take life seriously, and in my case to not take myself too seriously, so that I can be present to this moment. Then I can enjoy the glass of water I receive from the tap. I pause to listen to the voice at the other end of the phone call, or text message. I welcome the song of a bird, and the warmth of the sun, and the soft gentle rain for my garden. I breathe into the moment and receive the gift it offers me. All of our decisions reflect some form of relationship, of connectedness.

When I was about seven, my mother chose to leave her first husband Steve. It was a difficult decision for her. She had a son with this man. She had tried to leave him once earlier because of his violence toward her. I remember they were in the kitchen each holding an arm and a leg, him refusing to let his son go with her. So, she stayed, because she couldn't leave my brother. Steve worked on the railroad and was away a month or more at a time. It was hard for her when he returned home because he was abusive toward her, often unkind and harsh. I remember an incident when I was about five when he had me between his knees, talking to me, while looking at my mother trying to convince me what an awful mother she was, wanting me to agree with him. I felt torn, helpless, and frightened by the anguish I saw on my mother's face. But when I'd been an infant, Steve had been her escape route. She'd had no support when I was born. She told me that for a short time she and I lived in a room at the railway station, which was where she, apparently, met Steve; marrying him gave her a home and him a partner.

A couple of years later, when I was about seven, she chose to leave with a new partner, John. This choice required that she leave my half-brother Stanley behind with a neighbour. He was about four. That was a terrible choice for her to have to make, and she made it.

Stanley always remained in my heart. When I was sixteen, I tried to connect with him by writing a letter, which he never was given. It wasn't until I presided at our mother's funeral that I met him again. He was tracked down by the RCMP to be notified of her death. He responded. I smiled inwardly when I first met him again. He looked like a bush man, blue jeans, green work shirt, and a baseball cap. It was good to see him again, and to meet his wife, Lois. I met two good solid people that day and I felt again the inner bond and connection I had always carried toward him. At least forty-five years had passed, and his goodness had never left me. I had not forgotten him.

Life offers choices every day. Even in front of indifference, pain, and suffering, there are offerings of joy and goodness, moments of quiet and solitude. All of these are opportunities to respond to grace, Sacred Presence, life or death. In each of us is written the invitation to wholeness, to live love, to unveil truth, respond to a holy dreaming. Each of us are fashioned by our decisions, by our relationships, by our responses to life's offerings. Each of us carry grace and purpose for this time. In chapter 22 you will find an examination of consciousness that will invite you to a practice of daily reflection, to be aware of your options.

As I write, today is the second Sunday of Lent. Lent, in the Ukrainian Catholic tradition, means "bright spring." This is the second Sunday of waiting for the light of spring to awaken us to another level of consciousness, to take our place on this planet as wakeful people of justice, compassion, and mercy. The two Scriptural readings that surround this Sunday are Abraham preparing to sacrifice Isaac, and the Transfiguration of Jesus.[4]

I find the Abraham Old Testament passage challenging to read from my present perspective. So, I offer the following interpretation. Abraham is known as the father of faith. He is foundational to the emergence of what Jesus—and we as Christians—have come to believe. Somewhere in his life, Abraham had a God seizure, a mystical experience that he built his life around. In the intention of sacrificing his son, Isaac, I suspect he had another experience that led him to a deeper understanding of the God he believed in, this one of compassion and mercy.

The second passage from the New Testament takes place on the mountain of the Transfiguration. Here we see depicted two Old

---

4  In the Byzantine tradition, we have an icon reflecting the mystical reality of the Transfiguration. When we were illiterate, we were taught scripture through icons. If you have been in Eastern Orthodox churches, Byzantine churches, you would have seen icons written on the sacred doors, the ceilings, and walls which invite the people to prayer and reflection. The icon is written (painted), and is a reflection of the sacred, inviting the person to gaze, and be drawn into revelation given through what emanates from beyond the image to finally be led into who and what we are as sacred image.

Testament prophets with Jesus, reflecting on the lineage given to Jesus and making visible something of his own transformation, and his mystical experience to his disciples.

Our journey, our life integration is meant to bring us to living a radiance of transformation. The faithfulness of Jesus, the continued release of the sacred impulse living and moving in him, is meant to be our journey. Our journey entails integrating the events of our lives, gathering the insights and the grace, moving through the challenges, the sufferings, the good and bad relationships, learning from and through the events that have shaped us, to the point to standing well in ourselves as transparent gifts of life to the world.

# CHAPTER 9:
# Memory

IN MY UKRAINIAN Catholic tradition, when someone dies, we commend them to Eternal Memory, to that Sacred Realm where everything of our lived love and life is held by sacred knowing and presence. In holding our lived life, the life that we carry from day to day, it is sometimes helpful to gather our memories, especially those memories that name us in our goodness, as well as those that expose particular elements of suffering that need to be looked at and dealt with so that they don't interfere with our growing graciously into old age.

There are memories that become buried until we are strong enough to deal with the pain that is hidden there. There are memories that speak of our courage, our strength, our capacity to face what seems impossible. Sometimes it is helpful to do a timeline of our history: where we lived, what events, situations called us forth, diminished us, fashioned our values, awakened our dreams, insisted that we choose, choose something that was for life in us. In remembering, it is important to gather the memories of the people who have influenced our lives, what they awakened in us, affirmed in us, challenged in us, diminished in us, so that we can free the life locked there, and what of them and their goodness continues to resonate in us, surfacing unannounced to be wrapped in fondness.

Working with memories helps clarify the feelings that awaken, because the feelings can make memory live as if the moment is now. That's what makes trauma work so challenging. And that's why we need accompaniment, because we need to be held in the present to work with the past. We need to learn to hold ourselves in the present so that we can harvest the strength we relied on to be here today. Choose memories that you have learned from to gather your inner learnings.

For example, I spoke earlier of myself as a fourteen/fifteen-year-old, at home caring for my mother and my half siblings, and deciding I needed to get a job, and to find a way to go back to school. I had read as much of the local library as I could, and being home wasn't enough for me. I spoke of getting a job at the local hotel café. Besides the manager who was the cook, I was the only staff. Of the hotel patrons, I would try to guess who were the coffee, tea, and milk drinkers. It was fun to reach into my intuition to see when I was right. On the way home I would often take a long cut and do story time for some young children in the block, who would sit and wait for me. Then off home I'd go to tend to my responsibilities there. I did that until I was offered the job in Osoyoos to waitress at another hotel café.

Now I take this memory of this time in my teenaged life and break it down: What did I lean on, rely on in myself to move into the future? I come back to this Sacred Thread that was rooted in wisdom. Looking back, I had courage, joy, openness, and inner seeing that fed my intuition, desire to do and be more than what filled my life; I also had imagination at the time, hope and anticipation that came from my inner dreamer. All of these carried energy and determination, sometimes expressed as stubbornness or wilfulness. But also, the relationship with children kept my wonder alive and my inner innocence available to deepen my search for the sacred. Memories and events are full of possibilities to gather and receive what names us, builds us, and sends us forth. Part of our journey is to plumb these memories. They carry the building blocks of our present selves.

Previously I spoke of sitting before an RCMP constable and being told I needed to be obedient to my mother. I protected her by refusing to defend myself or accuse her. The reason I didn't speak up on this occasion was because when I was about twelve my mother overdosed, and I shared the incident with a neighbour. It was awful for me, and I needed to tell someone. However, my mother found out that I had told our neighbour. She felt ashamed and judged and betrayed by me. She asked me how I could tell someone about the incident, how in her mind I could speak badly of her. How could I diminish her? I never did that again, as much as I may have wanted to. Later, as I worked though some of the pain of my history, I spoke of her. I spoke of her expectations of me, of the feeling of her not being there for me. But I didn't condemn her. All of that took some years, and finally one day, I saw the humanity of my mother. I saw what she herself never had and understood how it was that she couldn't give me what I needed from her.

Anyway, continuing my story, I went to live with my mother, stepfather and four siblings.

I started my ninth grade at the local school in Keremeos, found two part-time jobs after school, and proceeded to push the boundaries by giving only a small amount of my earnings to help the family. Poverty is such a big trap, with very few exit doors. My stepfather worked on and off, not because he didn't want to work, but because it seemed there wasn't a lot for work for him. Needless to say, what little I earned was coveted, and I didn't want to share as much as was needed. So, one day, my mother and I had a big argument around the issue. That's when I heard my stepfather say, "Either she goes, or I go." And that was it for me! I stayed with my stepfather's mother for a couple of weeks, until she was told by one of her daughters that she would lose her pension if I continued to stay there. Then I boarded a bus and went to live with a friend until I found a room in a rooming house, went to school, and got a job, until the next chapter—involving nursing—began.

On days with space, I would hang out the window of my room in the rooming house and play the only three chords I knew on my little, old, cheap guitar and sing my heart out. I had an interior place that refused to die. I bent into my strength and bent into the future, somehow trusting there was something there. I was capable and able to intuit ways of managing what little I had, and I was determined to get an education, determined to live, determined to find a way into life.

Again, I relied on that strong, invisible thread of life that was given as promise. I sought out people mostly women, who were women of faith, of goodness, who were stable, and were learned, and some of whom were professional. In training, it was the nurses, and some housekeeping staff. When in school, it was teachers. At church it was a couple of priests and some of the faith community. Of course, I grappled with loneliness, with self-pity, anger, hatred, and being alone, feeling that I had no one that I could rely on, or to fall back on. I found it hard not having family that supported me. There were times when I found it hard to live and wished I would just not wake up—yet I refused to die.

I was also always "falling in love" with people. I fell in love with goodness. I tended to find it in people and put my trust in it. I also put my own goodness out there to help, to do, to play. And too often my goodness ran ahead of me, so that I gave too much, tried too hard, and still felt alone, unmet, and unknown. Once I got over the sense of my mother's rejection and my rejection of her, I realized I learned to live that kind of goodness from her. She carried that kind of generosity, that kind of innocence and naivete. Her goodness and generosity were always available to people, even though she was needy and wounded by not having what she needed to feel valued as a woman and a human being. As my memory clarified and was washed through aging and healing, I came to terms with what my mother couldn't be and received what she could. I realized that the memory of my innocent self held the sacred reality out of which I had come, and my memory of God's invitation to be. I met my mother's own profound sacredness and beauty through a visitation after her death. In that experience, I was able to know what I had never seen or known of her. And so I commend her again to sacred memory.

# CHAPTER 10:
# Trusting Sacred Revelation

THE QUESTION FOR the moment is: How do we get to this knowing of sacredness? What tools do we need, who do we need, what kind of relationship, community do we need to help that happen?

Only in the availability to the moment can we be drawn into grace and see, hear, and feel the beating heart of life that can change our perceptions and ease our breath to be released into what is before us, be it walking down the driveway, or noticing the stirring of life beneath the last traces of winter. The sacred is within us. God, Sacred Mystery, comes to us there, in the moment, often when we least expect and always when we are most in need.

When I was young, I tried to figure out what kind of God was all knowing, all seeing, kind of like a Santa Claus, where if I was good enough, prayed hard enough, "He" (it was always he) would answer my prayer, and look after me. Or the God who was like a magician would magically come to the rescue and fix things, if I just tried harder. But this sacred reality is much bigger and much simpler than that. Everything of God, sacred emergence, self-revelation, is relationship.

And so, that sacred thread that I held onto, this ever-present reality of love that rooted itself in me, saved me. I trusted this relationship; I didn't fully trust or believe my relationships with people, but I trusted and believed this thread. I believed in it without having had any great knowledge of religion, or God. I believed in something more, knew something more even though I couldn't explain how I knew it. It was something in my nature. It was also something in my mother's nature, though I'm not sure she would have been able to articulate it. One clue for me though, was a day I dropped bread on the floor, and she said, "Be careful with bread—don't leave it on the floor. It is holy."

In my years of reflection, I have had to examine again and again my image of Sacred Mystery, of God. I moved from knowing the God of distant places, the One who recorded my every thought, my every behaviour—especially those actions that judged my wanting— to the One who abounds in love and mercy. I had to move from the God I heard about in religious talk, to the reality that infuses the whole of life, the whole of creation, longing for all to be revealed in its goodness and sacredness. I tended to live with an image of God that judged on the outside, and with the One who held me precious on the inside. And it was through this inner meeting and knowing that I finally came to understand the God Jesus spoke to, for, and about—this deep reality of Sacred Presence. We all need to come to terms with what kind of god/God we believe in. What power we give our lives to. Who or what we place our trust in?

As I said earlier, I believed education would save me. When I finally got to university, I thought I would finally have a significant place in the world. Education would give me importance, status, acceptance through the accumulation of words from gathered information. In my second year of studies, I moved into a place of great disillusionment. I had no idea where God was in my life, what held my life together, what I was doing at this great school of study. I went to class and felt the great emptiness of the illusion I had built a part of my life on. I walked and felt the earth beneath my feet like sawdust, no life in it.

In fact, I was deeply depressed. On clearer days, I was grateful, because there were wonderful people around me who reached out to me, supported me, made sure I ate, encouraged me as I continued to follow my classes. One day, I woke to the realization that education was a tool, not something that would save me. It was a means for opening life, empowering it, and carrying the capacity to call it forth. It wasn't what I was meant to give my heart to but to use my heart for to see a bigger world, to learn to read from a deeper book, to find a path that availed me to learn the way of sacredness and follow it.

Upon surfacing, I became involved in youth retreats. I helped out with cooking for a house of Sisters who had lost their cook, and I wept for having come so close to being lost to a sense of meaning. But, amazingly, the following year, I graduated with my first degree. Pauline Vanier was the chancellor of the University of Ottawa at that time. I had come to know her somewhat, through correspondence, and other activities I was involved in, and it was she who handed me my degree with a "bravo!"

As I have said previously, if you have carried and lived self-pity you will have recognized what a thief it can be, robbing oneself of the good that resides at a deeper level. Self-pity can appropriate life, take possession of it, and dig a hole, making room for darkness that isolates and depresses, pushes down out of sight what gives life or where it might be found. Self-pity holds on to suffering, fuels anger and resentment, lingers in comparisons, carries a measuring stick of not-enoughness, and ultimately robs us of life, denying the expressions of care and love. All of this is different from being saddened, or weeping in grief, for loss of what wasn't given (also grieving for what could, and even should have been, and wasn't).

Grief allows us to wail, to reflect, to talk, and gather strength for what the journey holds at that point. Grief allows us to withdraw and stare into what appears to be nothing, waiting for some form of revelation. Alternatively, we work frenetically at something, anything, till we are tired of the distraction, and hold the pain to release its grace. I used the phrase "just you and me, Jesus" often in my young life. It is what I said when my stepfather told my mother, "Either she goes, or I go," as I was packed up and going out the door of our small, four-room house.

When I finally worked through the pain of that moment in my life, in my forties, I found that statement to be my stepfather's greatest gift to me, for without it, I never would have found my way to all of that which has challenged me, blessed my life, and come to know.

*A shadow between light and darkness, I stood alone.*
*The crags of emptiness carved my burning self into nothingness.*
*I looked about me, but all was hollow, still, nothing.*
*I walked and the earth clung to the bareness of my skin while rocks*
*like broken glass ground their way into my gaping flesh.*
*I stopped to soothe my wounds with tears that flowed like torrents*
*from a broken river.*
*But what healing could I do?*
*I was alone.*
*A shadow between light and darkness.*
*Stumbling, falling, crying, alone, I walked again.*
*Reaching, searching, groping blind.*
*But all seemed lost. Futility.*
*A breath, a faltering step—*
*a mangled garbage of humanity,*
*I fell. And all was darkness deep and still.*
*Then*
*the dew of gentle fingers soothed my brow*
*and cleansed my wounds*
*and touched the darkness.*
*The sun bathed my naked body like honey from a golden vine.*
*I reached out and gentle fingers touched me.*
*And I was whole.*
*I looked*

*shy, a little afraid*
*awed, yet daring to hope*
*and saw you who are my friend.*

*–March 1970*

I have been so grateful for all the friendships I have known, been changed by, grieved by, lost. They have led me more and more deeply into what I have come to know and understand from Eucharist, what Jesus meant by the sacrament of community and friendship, what John Dominic Crossan (1991) named as the *Companionship of Empowerment*. This has invited me to be available to the unfathomable bigness of what is at the heart of creation. Unnameable mystery.

God is in all, moves in all, speaks in all. The whole journey into the sacred is a journey of integration. It isn't just God and me. It isn't just you and me. It is all about relationship with self, others, reality, and the sacred. Each of these pathways must be integrated into the place of wholeness in us. So, we learn to be attentive, we learn to read what we carry within our feelings, our reactions, our dreams, our illusions, our responses, so that we can name our intentions, sift, sort, and choose what we want to live.

This sounds like a lot of work. It is big work yes, but it is not all-at-once work. It is process work. It is befriending ourselves for the journey, and the journey work. It is being attentive to the drawing of sacred knowing that moves toward us, desiring us to embrace the promise of what isn't yet and can be because we live. The Sacred Creative Genius is not a bystander watching us muck around with life, but an integral part of evolution, surprising us often through the intuitive meeting of hearts and minds and spirit. Often, we are surprised to receive a call or text—seemingly out of the blue—from someone we were just thinking of. At other times, when things come together out of holy synchronicity, or times in moments of desperation, it feels like the sky mysteriously opens. Those are moments that feel like a sacred intervention, of Sacred Mystery—this mystery out of which we have come, have emerged, this Sacred Mystery that somehow decided to burst itself into matter, because without matter it has no expression, because without matter it carries no expressed purpose. Without matter, there is no incarnation of wisdom, of the Christ presence, or the unveiling of journey, or the grace of relationship. All of this is at the heart of a spiritual journey that shapes our beliefs and opens up our availability to know and experience the sacred. The new sciences are pulling together the wonders of the universe and creation. These new discoveries continue to introduce me to the vastness and marvels of this universe. These continue to nourish the seeker in me, to affirm what I have come to know, and to fill me with wonder and radical amazement. Sacred Mystery is always living the inherent genius of self-revelation. It is at the heart of mysticism, which unfolds my sense of oneness with all that is allowing me to participate in the process of birthing the not-yet.

> *I spent the morning on Sunday helping to prepare the readings for a liturgy for a friend's father's funeral. It was good. I found in me the invitation to spend the rest of the day in prayer. I went outside and sat with my journal, my scriptures, and a book that I was reading. By and by, a dragonfly landed on the fence near the roses. I decided to go and look at him/her, since this wonderful creature of God helps with the mosquitoes that have been taking parts of me with them as I work in the garden. I thought in front of this wonderful creation: "Will you be here long enough that I can get my camera?" At that moment, it flew. Out of the corner of my eye I noticed something land on my upper arm, quite near my shoulder. I was tempted to sweep it away simply out of a reflex reaction to bugs. But I looked. And to my amazement the dragonfly had settled itself on my sleeve. It had a large wingspan, and a thick, long body. It really looked well fed. My heart filled with delight. The wind came up in strong gusts that day.*
>
> *And so began my teaching.*

*The gust of wind came and pushed against this creature of God. Its wings lifted and its legs pulled further into my shirt so that I could feel them hold almost to my skin. Slowly this seemingly weightless creation began to take weight and carry a mass of energy. It grounded itself into my own life and body and held firm. Then as the wind lifted and relaxed, this creature again became weightless. Until the wind again rose. And so it went as I made my way back into my chair. I read and I watched and occasionally talked to this creation on my arm. Amazed that it would stay. But only long enough until I heard its message within me: "Ground yourself in Life, in Love, in Spirit. Then you will not have to resist the wind. You will have the power and strength to endure it."*

– June 15, 1995

# CHAPTER 11:
## Awakening to the Sacred

*To hold the mystery and to take hold of the revelation.*
*Bending into timelessness for the naming that is given from the level*
*of soul*
*where the sifting and sorting is made for the emergence of wisdom.*
*To keep the mind still enough in silence and,*
*on the other side of that, to abandon the need to control it.*
*To detach from its wanderings and simply focus on the silence*
*that is so often full of gifting.*
*And*
*The Word, this sacred energy charged with power and grace,*
*was made flesh—I experience it resonate in mine—*
*naming me in a new way . . .*

*this God who comes,*
*blessing and unveiling . . .*
*sending . . . enfleshing . . . Love.*

*– October 15, 1995*

ALL MY LIFE I have been attracted to the sacred, to people who reflected believing in something of the more that I hadn't named yet or been wrapped in. In my young life, those who attracted me the most, assured me the most, were women of faith, some of whom were in religious life, and others who were single and committed to some form of service. Also, there were a few priests who encouraged my own inner priesthood to emerge and live eucharist and be bread of life for the world. It wasn't so much that most of these were Catholic, though Catholicism gave a foundational context to what they carried.

It was that they knew and believed and carried something that pointed to a way of living and being that carried a greater reality. Being part of a sacred tradition was part of it. My hunger and curiosity to know more, to be more, was an inner force that motivated me. And in my heart, I believed that I was made for something big, some big dreaming and unveiling. Perhaps you understand that inner sensation of life being so big that there isn't enough room inside to contain it.

There were times when I experienced it as a push at the walls of my soul, a push to speak, to create, to know something that was just at the edge of revelation. My music was born out of that. Songs, poetry came out of this dreaming and birthing and knowing. I would find myself waiting until it was time. And then I would receive what was given. I would write, I would sing, I would dance, I would weep. And so it was with my search for God, for the sacred and knowing one.

My formation toward adulthood was somewhat unconventional. I learned to live at the centre of life and at the edge of it, always imperfectly, always as authentically as my wounded, seeking, loving self could live. I learned to believe that there was almost nothing I

65

couldn't do. If it needed to be done, and I thought I could do it, I did it. When I was a student nurse, I had an elderly patient whose bed squealed terribly when I turned the crank to raise the head. I wrote up a number of requisitions to maintenance to deal with it. Finally, one day I got a jar of Vaseline, climbed under the bed in full uniform and dealt with it. While I was under there, my instructress came looking for me, and I got one of many lectures on conducting myself more professionally.

Because I sang on radio, people recognized my voice and called me by my first name. This too was called unprofessional. While working on pediatrics, a little child with Down's syndrome knocked his radio off the bedstand and it fell apart. I fixed it, and ever after, each time I arrived on the floor, a little body ran toward me and hugged me. He brought such delight and joy to my heart. I was not proper, according to standards of professional behaviour. I was, however, caring and patient-oriented. I sang children to sleep, I soothed sleepless patients with back rubs and silent prayer. And I was loved. I appreciated being in front of that reality, it was good for me, it strengthened me. Not all of me knew how to let it in, how to believe in being loved, but I hung out with it, until I could close my ever-ready exit door.

While I was still trying to get enough high school courses under my belt to qualify for university, I went to hear a woman give a presentation on nursing from the school of nursing in Edmonton. I wondered about continuing on in nursing. I met with this woman a number of times to explore the possibility. We had wonderful conversations wherein she introduced me to Aristotle, Michelangelo through the book *The Agony and the Ecstasy* by Stone. She lent me books by Francis Bacon, and one by Eleanor Roosevelt. We talked about Dostoyevsky's writings. My intellectual horizons were broadened, and still I made no decision to go on in nursing.

It wasn't until I was working evenings and nights on a pediatric ward as an LPN that I began to think about psychology. I saw so many sick children returning repeatedly and wondered what was at the root of this vulnerability. The seed was planted, and I would travel a number of miles before I found my way to watering it.

Edmonton was a significant city in my journey. After completing my master's degree in educational counselling, I returned to Edmonton with the intention of finding a job. I put out several job applications and found I was either overqualified or under qualified. And having studied in Ontario, at the University of Ottawa, and with further studies at the University of Arizona in Tucson, the government of Alberta wouldn't permit me to work in the school system without a B.Ed. I worked in social services for a period, as there was a government initiative program that I was hired to do some programming in. Then I finally went to the University of Alberta to get a teaching diploma.

It was one of those mucking-around periods of my life when being attentive to various opportunities was the order of the day. But nothing of life was lost in this mucking-around period. I volunteered and gave courses in adult-child relationships. I gave workshops to physiotherapists at the Glen Rose Hospital. And I formed many good and lasting friendships. And I did get work in the Catholic school system, where I taught fifth grade and was an elementary school counsellor. I lived in an apartment for a time, then lived at a house of prayer for a period and was the bread maker for those going into solitude. I lived with the Sisters of Holy Cross for a period while I was deciding if I would join them as a member. I began giving days of reflection to religious congregations and directing retreats. Edmonton was a place for cultivating my inner soil.

In 1968, when I finished my undergraduate studies, I was hired as a religious ed consultant for the Pembroke Separate School system. While I had done a fair bit of retreat work with youth, I had no real idea what it meant to be a consultant in four grades of religious education. I'm still amazed that they hired me for the position! I just remember being recommended for the position, and with the "of course I can" written into my survival code, I took the job. It took a month for the "Peter Principle" to hit me in the face. I met with the board and said, "I will not do this job justice, but if you really want me to use my gifts, let me offer retreats to the students."

I gave two retreats a day for thirty-nine schools, covering the whole diocese. What a privilege that was. I would have about two hundred students in the gym, morning and afternoon. Their attentiveness and responses were incredible for me. I had them learn to name themselves in their goodness and their uniqueness.

One exercise I used involved selecting an orange each. In groups they were to spend time with their orange to identify its uniqueness, then put it back in the box. They were grieved but did it. Then I asked them to find it again amid all the others. They had spent such concentrated time with their orange that when they did find it, they were delighted and relieved. They discovered uniqueness in all things. I also spent time with them in small groups. Reaching into my intuition, I would give them a colour, then tell them something of what I saw of them in their goodness. I saw their generosity, their curiosity, their ability to express care and their desire to be known. They thought I was somehow a mind reader, but I was just a seer and a reader of goodness. It was they who let me see who they were, and I simply reflected that back to them.

It was a wonderful year for me. And it carried a significant learning: when I drove onto the school yard, the yard would move with bodies toward my car. I became a hero symbol. And as I prayed around this each day, I found I had to be attentive to the authority I was being given, that it didn't become power. It was a deeply humbling and frightening realization. I had to discipline the ego big time. It could be so easy to take too much importance to myself. That was the danger in that time.

I often drove ninety km to Combermere for their once-a-week prayer meeting. Praying with a community was important for me. It's where I met the Baroness Catherine Doherty. She was a powerhouse of a woman. She minced no words nor was she hesitant in her expression of faith. It was a gift to pray with her and her community.

In this year with the diocese, I met a wonderful group of nuns called the Faithful Companions of Jesus. They had rented a cabin near the Combermere community called The Farm. Mary Malone was one of them, she and her religious Sister Sabina. I don't remember how long I spent with them; it was a few days. Long enough to be encouraged to record my first album, *I Wish You Rainbows*. Long enough to develop bonds that lasted.

Bonds of friendship allow us to weave in and out of each other's lives forever. Bonds allow us to spend an hour or two after years apart and feel as though it was yesterday that we sat and talked. Bonds allow for the sharing of life at a level that always has space. There's space for compassion, for shared joy, for receiving the pain of grief, for continued dreaming into old age, and for unveiling again and again Sacred Mystery that unfolds the continued promise of life unknown and deeply familiar. In these bonds of friendship, we are never strangers but companions on this one journey given to share.

This year with the Pembroke school board was full of grace. I was then "borrowed" by the Souris Prince Edward Island Education Department. I went there during spring break and gathered young people from the area. It was the season of coffee houses, and I often sang in them, or was asked to do concerts for fundraising for missions in India. There are so many things I would not have done had I not heard, "Either she goes, or I go."

Following this year of so much gift, I went back to the University of Ottawa and worked toward my masters. As everyone knows, university is costly. My savings only went so far, both for the first degree and for the masters. When I ran out of funds in the first degree, a friend asked her father to lend me enough money to finish it. He did. For the masters, before I could withdraw, the Sister in leadership of the Sisters of St. Joseph of Pembroke called me and told me they would lend me what I needed to finish. I suppose in some way, I became a child of the universe, belonging to no one and being related to everyone. And ultimately belonging to God.

There is a passage I found once when I was working through some very deep, painful history. This passage is from Ezekiel 16:

4-10. I will only use a couple of lines here because that is all that is required for me at this point. It reads like this: "I saw you as I was passing. Your time had come. The time for love. I bathed you in water, I washed the blood off of you. I spread my cloak over you, I anointed you with oil. I gave you my oath, made a covenant with you and you became mine."

*Holy God creator of my heart*
*I thank you for life, for love, for rediscovery.*
*I thank you for all that has been, for all that will be.*
*Always one, always faithful Grace*
*You are Gracious God of my heart.*
*I thank you for your goodness to me.*
*Tenderness guides me,*
*holding me,*
*gifting me to the world.*
*Strongly-rooted-God it is you who hold me.*
*In you I belong, with You I am home.*
*Beloved God of my heart, I thank you.*
*You have blessed me.*

*– July 1989*

On December 13th, 1986, I recorded a deep gift while spending the day in my hermitage. Sometimes working through our inner sacred wound, that marking of our innocence and trust, is big work. It was for me. In this day of prayer, I had a "visitation by Grace." I was given the invitation to realize that God brought me to my moment of conception with reverence and delight, as a gift to be welcomed and received, with the consciousness of God that is written in each of our souls. But when I came to my mother and father's family out of wedlock, I was met with horror and rejection, because my existence brought shame on them. This shame entered and cut my heart and severed my sacredness except for the fine thread that kept me connected to the deepest part of my being and that carried my goodness and original innocence. Shame caused my mother to be beaten in an effort to abort me. And shame marked me by the judgment that others carried toward me, that I believed. I learned to believe that I was despicable, that I was destined to give love, be in front of love, but not have it for me. This fine thread of life that awakened itself so powerfully and specifically to the fourth/fifth grader contradicted the lie that I was a mistake. This sacred thread became hidden beneath the lie, but fortunately the trust that was encased in this fine thread of life would often lie open in my significant relationships, with something of a twist. My maturing self would be watchful, careful, protective, as well as receptive. At times I would also be reckless, trusting too much, giving too much, believing too much, entrusting too much. And all the while I was being fashioned to grow in wisdom and grace.

This day of visitation and grace, this moment of deep Sacred Presence, holding me rooted in timelessness, meant reaching through the pain of my history and receiving myself as God intended: to be reverent with my life, to receive the gift of it, to offer it as a gift that carried intention and purpose. I was empowered to continue the work of letting go of unmet expectations, to name and discern the needs I needed to care for, rather than wait for someone else to meet them. This moment wasn't the end of my healing, but it stood me up enough so that I could rest in myself, work toward the end of it, evict the lie that encrusted a significant point of my innocence and goodness. We are meant to heal, you know. We are made to stand fully in ourselves even as we limp along, because we are more than our woundedness. Sometimes we give up our future by clinging to our past and so we haven't fully emerged into all that we can be and are meant to do. We need to activate and exercise the courage we are given for life, to choose life, and to be attentive to bring life. This is not an act of willpower. It is a decision in fidelity, in faithfulness, to the deepest longing and knowing of our heart. Fidelity is a disposition, a commitment, that helps to hold what is true, no more and no less, that is necessary for the journey. This is where a listener, a therapist, a community, the journal, can call us to authenticity.

*Father God, guide my heart as you guide creation in the way of
your love.*
*Mother God, breathe softness into this day before me, breathe softness
into me,*
*that I may access wisdom and respect in my response to who and
what I meet.*
*Your eyes of love filled with compassion:*
*Awaken eyes of love in me.*
*Your heart of love filled with the desire for truth and understanding:*
*Awaken discernment within me.*
*Your Presence of Love strong and unwavering:*
*Root me in my strength and your Presence in me.*
*Hold me in wakefulness where we are one*
*That I in my littleness may be as you are.*

*– July 20, 1993*

When we have the courage to embrace the gift and grace of our lives, we are invited to be in relation with all of it. We learn to bend into it, be attentive to what writes itself there for our understanding and learning, and in listening and receiving, read what moves and becomes written there as gift. In some of my journal gatherings I found rules I had written for myself as protection and for survival. Keep in mind that children are good perceivers but poor interpreters. Children don't miss a lot of what goes on around them. They are sponges, always taking things in. And so it was with me in my early life.

My sensitivity was honed and fashioned by my mother's need, her loneliness, her playfulness, her love of music, dancing, and her perfectionism. I was my mother's dance partner for the polka when I was five, sang "Goodnight Irene" and "You Are My Sunshine" and whatever other country songs were in her repertoire at the time. And she had high expectations of me, so that I decided I had to get things right the first-time round. My interpretations wrote my rules. So why is it important to be able to know the rules that govern our perceptions and interpretations? Because they form our ethics, our rigidity, our boundaries, or lack thereof. They fashion our defenses, and they can keep us from our deepest freedom. That is because often they bypass the heart and keep us in our head. So, we need some tools.

One of my most significant and helpful tools is the journal. It is the place I have written most of what I have lived and sought to understand. Some of it is deeply insightful, and moving, and some sheer yuck. Some of the yuck has brought up old shame, and judgement, and a desire to run away from who I was then, in that time of learning. And I have had to accept my lack of knowing and integration, forgive what I was and couldn't be. It is a humbling task to take this human journey seriously, to become fully human, fully who we are invited to become for the emergence of life, the revelation of grace.

# CHAPTER 12:
## Embracing Aloneness

BECAUSE I BELIEVED very early in my life that I was destined to wander the universe giving love, being caring without any of it for me, I hid in a place called "Alone." Alone tried to keep me safe. One of the rules it carried for me was not to ask for much, not show need, real need. Being self-sufficient was a virtue, that meant not needing anyone: making it on my own. Of course, what that also meant is that when something real and true was offered, it got missed because there has to be receptivity and inner space in order to receive. This is where many people starve to death because of inner blindness and self-enclosure.

When I was befriending "Aloneness" in me, I wrote: "I need to allow myself to be at the "mercy" of others, I need to allow them to exercise their mercy and goodness toward me, to care for me." I needed to open my hiding place a crack so that I could be found, called out, and receive. Scary business, that! This is where having a spiritual accompanier is very helpful, and in some life moments essential. Being marked by "Aloneness" didn't tell me the truth about myself as loveable, and good. I had to let others in to help heal that place in me. And I had to go there fully myself, walk around in it, and receive the life that was locked in it. What I found there at the bottom of the Aloneness was that the One who called me into life, the ultimate Sacred Presence, was there waiting for me, and that I had never been alone. I had always been held in love. Always held in Oneness. The core belief of my Aloneness was that I had to make it on my own. It was a lie. A lie isn't converted, it is simply no longer believed.

Having said all of the above: What was the gift to me, in and through Aloneness? I developed my capacity to see. I could wonder at the beauty of a sunset, or the fragrance of a rose. I could watch for goodness in people, delight in children and allow myself to crawl around the floor playing hide-and-seek and be able to giggle and laugh because I could. I learned to play the guitar by watching others finger the frets so that I could sing loud and express some of my wildness. I developed my creativity, and I was able to do with little without being a minimalist, even though there were times that I was. I learned to build things; I couldn't afford to buy a desk as a student, so I built a table. When I finished university, and I wanted to pay back the money so generously lent me, my apartment was barren. I slept on a mattress on the floor. When I had guests for dinner, I spread a tablecloth on the floor and served my guests there. I did as much maintenance of my vehicles as I could, like changing the oil and sparkplugs—when cars had such things. And I developed a heart of gratitude.

Gratitude allowed me to live each day receiving gifts and blessing and to live joy. Aloneness carried my wound. It also challenged me to not settle for the least in life. Robert Browning said, "Your reach must be beyond your grasp, or what is a heaven for?" I had to decide somewhere in the process what it was that I wanted, and what I needed to do to get there, and who I wanted to be part of that, as best as I could. Some people dropped in temporarily as guests and others were great cultivators of the possible for me and in me, and lived into my future, sharing dreams, and exploring the possible.

Aloneness hid me until I was strong enough to come out of hiding and be seen and loved for who I was. Emptied of Aloneness, I was able to live from my deepest freedom, and give myself even more fully to the dream of God living in me and around me at the heart of All-Beginnings—an essential aspect of my big journey.

In the midst of all these years, I found myself listening to my God-belongingness, and thought I would seek a community that met what I carried inside. I woke from a dream one morning that had me knocking on doors. Someone would come to the door and say it must have been the wind. Then finally, someone answered and invited me in. Working through the dream, I found it invited me to explore what it was that I would look for in a religious community. I wrote out my expectations, my vision for religious life, and what I myself was prepared to bring to it. Then I proceeded to make appointments with women in leadership so that I could ask them what their vision was, what they as a community were living and then share what I was looking for.

As I approached the entrance to the building of the last stop on my list, I found myself trembling. I was nervous and had a strong sense of something. I was led into a small parlour, and the person who came to meet me was barefoot, with long hair, and full of graciousness. She did not look like a nun to me, and as we talked, and she responded to my questions, it was as if she had read every line on my page of seeking and desiring. Over time we met, talked, shared tea in my furniture-less apartment, and we decided I would live with them and discern if that is where I would put my life. It was a French community, so I began to learn some French, and since I worked in a Catholic School system, I would be around the community in the evenings and weekends. In addition, I gave retreats/workshops to physiotherapists and other small groups of seekers.

I was also asked to give several one-day reflections to a community of Sisters who ran a hospital in a small town. In the summer of 1975, this community was going to have a general assembly for renewal. The speaker/facilitator that was to come became ill, so they asked if I would consider it. In my discernment, I came to realize that I was not meant for religious life, but to work with religious without being a member of any congregation. I said yes to the invitation, which took on its own life. It was the beginning of immersing myself in religious life, in the gospel, in following not only my inner journey but the journey of many working toward dreams, unravelling histories wrapped in grace, woundedness, as well as liberation, and coming to understand something of what St. Paul meant when he said, "It is a fearful (and awesome) thing to fall into the hands of the living God" (Hebrews 10:31). It is there that we find our way to Sacred Mystery, to community, to healing, to love, to friendships, to bring ourselves into the service of the whole to leave blessing in our stead and contribute to the not-yet of the future.

I have learned that the future runs toward us as grace, inviting us to be awake and available for the gift of our creation, which is necessary for its emergence. We are indeed part of this creative genius out of which we have been fashioned. During one of my camping prayer days in my twenties, I was invited to enter this reality more fully when the image of Jesus came to me out of the silence and solitude inviting me, arms open, to not simply dip myself in his reality like a chocolate-dipped marshmallow, but to fully immerse myself, all the way. For some of us, the way into our humanity, into our fullness of being who we are, is through the archetype of Jesus. He disclosed through his deep contemplation, his deep plunge into the Sacred Presence of awesome mystery, the path to wholeness. He revealed the face of wisdom, of love, of inclusivity, of mercy and justice. And through this faithfulness he unleashed the sacred energy of the Christ, living and moving among us.

# CHAPTER 13:
## Compassionate Companionship

YOU WILL HAVE found, as you've been reading, that I have not been giving you a chronological account of my life but rather dipping in and out of years that carry invitation and learning. It is my learnings that I want to share with you, hidden in details and story. It is to invite you to explore your own lives, to claim the grace and gift, to unearth your own sacred impulse that led you to break out of faulty learning, self-hatred, and rejection. It is to invite you to pass through your own disillusionment, or propped up illusions, to find the gift of your life as offering, holding its goodness and incompleteness.

In his book *The Human Being,* Walter Wink writes: "What draws us to the sufferings of God's messengers is not perfection but broken wholeness."[5]

*We confine God to concepts and then fail to recognize the hiddenness*
*of God*
*in the simplest gestures of reality.*

*– March 1994*

We break into Sacred Presence every time we bend into our lived experience to bring compassion and tenderness out of a listening heart. We break into Sacred Presence each time we choose to find our part in a misunderstanding or choose kindness, to listen to someone we dislike. We break into Sacred Presence every time we listen and hear and understand beyond our reason and believe that which hasn't given us permission to fully know.

And so it was, the weekend I had offered to go and pray with a young Sister named Joan who had been diagnosed with cancer and was believed to be terminally ill. I had been directing a retreat with two Jesuits at a retreat centre and had noticed her sitting during that week. I knew her somewhat, and one day near the end of the retreat, I asked if she was okay. And she shared with me a dream she'd had the previous night that contained a black hearse, among other details I have forgotten. What she understood was that the cancer in her body was taking her life.

Following the retreat, I carried her in my heart. I was facilitating some workshops in community renewal and visioning for another religious community in the province, and somewhere in there decided to call her to ask how she was doing and if she needed anything. Following our conversation, I said I had a weekend coming up and would be happy to spend it in prayer with her as she prepared for exploratory surgery. She was involved in rural catechetics so had

---

5    Wink, Walter, *The Human Being Jesus and the Enigma of the Son of the Man*, 32.

access to a small motor home. We arranged to take the vehicle and set off for a time of prayer.

Now, I enjoy campfires, so I cooked steak over an open fire, and had brought red wine. In those days I rarely went anywhere to do any form of ministry without carrying the Eucharist, the Sacred Bread, in a little gold container called a pix. Some people might consider it sacrilegious, but I learned to trust the presence of holiness to do what I could not, to protect, to lead, and to heal.

Having tripped into my thirties a short time before and spending so much time listening to the lives of so many people, I could not rely on myself alone. In conversation with a priest, I was given permission to carry the Eucharist for very particular situations. I did this for a period of time until I found this reality resided in me, that it was in me and in the beyond of me, ever present and available. I found going to mass, receiving Eucharist in the context of community, strengthened me to continue my own journey again and again, to be sent from there again and again, to become what I eat through the breaking of the bread.

As Joan sat and ate, she went into terrible pain. I didn't recognize her being in pain until she said she needed to lie down. I watched her as she lay on the sitting space across from the table. Needless to say, I couldn't continue eating, so I went and knelt beside the bed and placed my hand on the area of her stomach that was so filled with pain. I just sat in stillness, and prayer, and after twenty minutes she said the pain was gone. It was then that we noticed that the wind had come up. The little motor home began to sway a bit in the wind, the hanging garbage cans in the empty park clanged, and both of us were seized with fear. And we both felt as though some presence of evil was trying to harass us. We both began to pray the name of Jesus out loud and a little frantically.

Of course, a heart seized by fear in the presence of evil cannot pray. It cannot hold presence to listen and discern and follow what is given as direction. I got up and handed Joan the pix which contained the Eucharist, we asked Mary the Mother of Jesus to come with angels and saints and surround this little vehicle, and we continued to pray. The wind didn't stop, nor did the cans stop clanging, but the motor home became still in the wind, and the interior filled with peace. We continued to pray. We prayed through the evening and into the night. During this time of prayer, we listened deeply. Joan experienced movement in her abdomen as if things were being moved around. This movement held us in prayer, waiting, praying, following, until it felt done for now.

The following day, she phoned her Sisters, and she was told the hospital had called and she was to report to the hospital because her surgery had been scheduled.

This process of our journey, Joan's journey, carried elements we didn't know how to get our minds around. We finally tracked down Francis McNutt, who'd had many experiences with the healing power in prayer and had a conversation with him. We were grateful for his affirmation in saying he believed what we were living was authentic and reflected his experience and understanding. And the path we were on was unique to Joan, listening and responding, holding the mystery, listening and responding, following what was given, looking at it again and again to be sure we weren't somehow fooling ourselves, or imagining things just because we might want something to be so.

There is no room for willpower in prayer. In this process there is only total abandonment. The question most present was: "How can this be, what does this mean, and what are we meant to do, how are we meant to be? What is the learning?" What I have since come to know and believe and understand is that in the deepest part of us, where we and Sacred Mystery are one, at the place where we are both limited and boundless, where we are continually invited to become fully human, where Holy Wisdom speaks to our heart again and again, where we are capable of living in Sacred Presence, our very stillness moves energy toward relationship. And in the presence of this point of meeting, healing can come, peace can come, newness is given. It is a reality that only the heart can understand. It is not logical. It is not head knowledge, nor a function of willpower. It is a deeper will, it is the will that belongs to docility, and to holy abandonment. This will lives with holy indifference and is available to obedience, that deep listening that opens a path piece by piece, step by step, opening itself to the future that is already moving toward us.

How is it that a hummingbird can know that the flower that just provided its nectar, will do so again in ten minutes? How is it that a flower can "hear" the hummingbird, or the bee, approaching and can prepare its offering of nourishment? How is it that the roots of one tree can know the need for water of its neighbouring tree and send it some? How can this be? And yet this is how it is, this is the relational reality of Sacred Presence out of which we have come and are invited into knowing. It is through this holy reality that we embody Spirit and incarnate the One who dreams us again and again into becoming fully human.

Joan had her surgery. They opened and closed her and didn't remove anything. And there was some puzzlement about where the doctor had originally thought the cancer was. She was given a limited time to live. She arranged to meet with her family to prepare them and asked me to be with her for their preparation. I remember a day when I sat in her room grappling with her news and cried out to God saying, "I don't understand, I have given my life to you, for you, what have I done or not done that this has happened to me?" As she continued to live, she entered deeply into her beliefs, her perceptions, her self expectations, her woundedness. She worked hard at coming to terms with her faulty beliefs of perfection. Some of it she did with me and as it became evident that we would be ministering together, she found someone wiser than I to follow this deep inner journey she was on.

I must admit that initially I was simply following her in her process. I never thought I would be part of her life, until she died. It took a couple of years before I really recognized it. And it was a journey of conversion and transformation for me as well. In my past I had had roommates, I had been part of a community, had been taken in by families, but on the whole lived alone most of my life. Forming community with another person who was deeply committed and rooted in God was both a privilege and a challenge. Theologically, and relationally we were very compatible. We worked well together. At the same time, we were very different. Our differences were often a point of negotiation and conflict. Fortunately, we became part of a community of faith and growth. There were eight to ten of us that gathered every year. In addition to taking retreat together for five days a year for ten years, we also supported, listened to each other, encouraged each other in these retreats, so that we could deal with our histories, and what got in the way of living well with integrity and truth. It was important for us to do our own work if we were going to accompany others as they did theirs. In a sense this reality was a form of midwifery, accompanying people to healing and wholeness. It was a big journey, and as with all of the events and relationships in my life, I would not have been fashioned and formed to be as I am today without them. I would not have found the way to gather the fragments of my life, reclaim my own gift so that again and again I could be given as service to the world.

Fortunately, I have had a hermitage in some form all of my life. In the place of solitude, of silence, I could be held in God, in Sacred Presence. It is there that I was taught, where I listened, where I prayed, and where I came to know the God who has held me always and continues to be Holy Mystery, Holy Invitation, Source of All Life.

Joan lived fourteen years beyond what was thought to be the original six months to a year. After a couple of years of going back to the cancer clinic every six months, her doctor said "Sister, whatever it is you are doing, keep doing it because it is obviously working."

Living the journey, following the inner reality, keeping relationships clear where and when and how that is possible, and having someone follow the journey with us is all part of the journey for personal liberation and the liberation of the Sacred and Holy Mystery. We are meant to bring to completion aspects of creation that require what is written in us as gift, and wisdom, and unveiled love. Our life has purpose. Our life carries gift and blessing. Our life is related to all that is, from the smallest flower to the furthest star. There is a passage in Isaiah (55:10-11) that speaks to me. It reads:

*For as the rain and the snow come down from heaven,*
*and do not return there until they have watered the earth,*
*making it bring forth and sprout,*
*giving seed to the sower and bread to the eater,*
*so shall my word be that goes out of my mouth;*
*it shall not return to me empty,*
*but it shall accomplish that which I purpose,*
*and succeed in the thing for which I sent it.*

Usually, women who are vowed within a congregation, live as part of their community in one of their community houses. It is unusual for a Sister or a nun, to live with a layperson outside of the community, unless it is specifically designated by the congregational leadership. For Joan, apart from a few close friends in her congregation with whom she shared, her congregation didn't fully understand her choice or the inner mandate she heard in herself to live community with me. I didn't fully understand it myself, but I knew I too had to follow the process. At the time when the healing process began, the congregational leader tried to insist she live in one of their own homes, but Joan said she couldn't. She had to stay with what she heard in her deepest self, even if she couldn't explain it. Eventually the leadership gave her permission to live apart from the community while she worked at her inner and physical healing.

Fortunately, she had another Sister who accompanied her in her journey, who herself was a religious, and heard and understood her soul. There are times when there is a real unreasonableness to the reality we know as God. This big Dreamer, this God, who affirms our path, nudging us when life challenges us so that we become fully who we are without the constraints or the rigidity of the ego.

*Eight a.m. this morning the phone rang, letting me*
*know that Joan's hospital bed was on its way. I got up*
*and prepared her room. Then made us some break-*
*fast. The bed arrived while we were eating. When it*

*was all set up, we both went together to her room, we both wept as we went. We were both moving toward embracing a new reality, one that we were preparing for and not quite ready for. The inevitability of death and the mystery of the dying time seems to suspend time. We need to live the process, and to stay in the moment so that nothing is lost.*

*We scrubbed the bed together. It was a ritual of celebration, grief and the "yes" to this next phase. I was aware as I worked that this bed may very well be the one she will die in. For both of us, somehow, it was a ritual of wrapping every inch of it in love and grace, a solemn ritual of real life.*

*Later I bought some flowers as a way of acknowledging this very significant event. I also bought a bird feeder to hang outside her bedroom window.*

– October 26, 1990

I learned that in the early stages of the dying time, as much as can be said is said, as much as can be reconciled is brought to the fore and the rest is put to rest in forgiveness and gratitude for life lived. Only presence remains. Presence during small walks, moments of recognition of beauty in sunshine or a blossoming flower. Presence to the grace in breathing life, of having lived life.

One of the big moments of living was one morning when Joan, in this lengthy process of dying, was in terrible pain. It was 5:00 a.m. I went to her room and asked if I could call her doctor who made house calls. She said no, it is too early. So, I sat by her bed, in front of her and her pain, and held her in love and prayer. I was powerless to change what was, but I was not helpless. I could live presence, compassion, sympathy. There are no words in this time, only presence. There is no trying to make things better, only holy silence and waiting. Our birthing process, the movement from the womb into the human journey of becoming, requires strength, courage, fortitude. So it is with the dying process. It is a solitary journey meant to be accompanied by those who sit and hold and accompany us, those who weep with us, grieve with us, let go with us.

In my commitment to being available so that Joan was not alone as she was dying, I chose what I knew was so much a part of my essence in listening and being present. I emptied myself, made my interior self totally available to this dying time in order to be available to whatever arose and to whom ever came that she had the energy to welcome. She was very loved and those who came lived the time with her well. All received the gift of grace available from this sacred journey.

It's years now, and even though I am back in relationship with members of the community, we have never gone back to that time. And I don't think it is necessary. There is an acceptance in our relationship, and it doesn't have to be any more than it is. Not everything gets resolved. And not everything needs to be. Some things we just leave with God, within the realm of the Sacred, to bring whatever learnings can be left within the universe to use for the cultivation of compassion and mercy. I must admit, I did hope to meet with the person who was in charge, the one who had been in charge, to break the silence. But it wasn't to be until the last week of Joan's life. I welcomed her and another Sister into our home, and when I greeted them, all was clear in me, all was free in me, as I sensed it was in them. I didn't need to say anything, only offer hospitality, and let the two of them be with Joan, to say goodbye to Joan.

I overheard the person in leadership say to Joan, "My dear Sister, is there anything that you want, that I can do?"

And Joan replied simply, "I just want to see Jesus."

Sometimes to live and breathe and move in the Sacred is all there is.

Christin Lore Weber writes:

> Dying stars send particles into the universe, and
> from these new worlds are formed. So we are made
> of star dust. It is in our blood and bones; in the air
> we breathe, in the rocks and seas and plants. We have

known this for a long time and only recently have we discovered that the dust from dying stars has the chemical composition of diamonds. The death of a star showers us with diamonds . . . If we refuse to admit the power of small losses, we will surely be overwhelmed by those that are great. [6]

---

6    Weber, Christin Lore, *Blessings: A Womanchrist Reflection on the Beatitudes*, (San Francisco: Harper and Row, Publishers, 1989), 39.

# CHAPTER 14:
## Passage in Grief and Absence

*I walked in the garden*
*And met the spirit of your footprints*
*Where you stood in wonder so many times before . . .*
*I met a part of your soul*
*And was grateful for the Earth in releasing that moment to*
*my consciousness.*

*– September 1993*

ABSENCE CARVED ITSELF out in me. I had to gather my listening self, my abandoned-available-to-the-journey self, that part of me that had been totally focused on the final journey and wait for whatever Sacred Mystery held in openness and invitation to me. I grappled with the aloneness that came with this time. I grappled with loss and all that went with it. I grappled with the guilt of not having been enough so often in years past, of not being fully present. And then in this time of absence, in so many ways I was hidden in myself, even as I tried to regather all I had put outside of myself. I worked at regrouping my introverted self as I lived, being present to those I accompanied, and to the groups who gathered, to the ones who came to further their growth. I honoured those who came to pray, and to integrate their memory of Joan and her dying time. For me, this time was ever deepening in the call to Holy Silence and stillness, availability, and response.

Absence always teaches, and has different faces. Death created an absence that led me through a whole passage and transformation. Separation carries another kind of absence. Absence is a holy space filled with grace. So always the question before it is: What learnings does it carry? The response isn't given intellectually, it arises from the soul. Absence creates space for longing to speak. God fills the absence in the same way Jesus experienced absence in the garden, on the cross, until God broke through into the resurrection, availing the Christ embrace to each of us within the whole of creation.

*A moment of Grace in time*
*A potter's hand moulding infinity as one*
*Moment upon moment*
*And mystery again*
*Breathless, fearless, and whole.*
*I saw you as the shadows faded*
*And life drew its veil over your face*
*I wondered if I would ever see you again*
*And to my surprise I see you*
*In the sun, and in the flowers*
*And in the gentle fall of snow.*
*And I remember.*
*A hand full of memories*
*A thousand years to know them.*

*– October 17, 1992*

And so, how to live absence. How to grapple with loss? Death is a natural process in life. Without it, there is no life, no newness, no emergence of the more. And even when we are prepared for it, it carries a surprise, a letting go and a moving in unfamiliarity. For me it wasn't the dying that was so grievous for me, it was the pain. How to be in the presence of so much physical pain and be powerless to change it. How to live the process well, to be available to hold the sacredness of the life in front of me, and to do all that I was meant to do, no more and no less.

Fortunately, Joan was strong in herself. When my fuss budget was activated, she would say, "Doreen, stop fussing, I will ask if I need something. I am capable and will do what I can until I can't anymore."

The challenge for many of us is how to be, and what to do in the presence of another's pain without making it our own. How to hold life softly, yet firmly, with an availability grounded in listening with the heart, and relying on Holy Wisdom to offer direction.

When someone dies in a family, in community, in friendship, or in any living relationship, there is absence. All who were part of our small living community had to embrace absence, loss, and be drawn into the future, hollowed out and called to the more.

Joan was very faithful to her life, did all that she could, no more and no less, every day. In her last year, she spent much of her day in her chair in the living room. She offered her chair-sleeping as prayer for those who came to the house for continued counselling and spiritual direction. I cut my work back to a third so that she would not be alone in her journey. I sat with her, sometimes read to her, took short walks with her to the end of the drive and back. Mostly I sat in quiet and stillness. We had one last retreat at our house with the group we'd met with every year over ten years. Raymond, an oblate priest, said to her, "You are showing us how to live the journey of dying in deep faithfulness, fully abandoned to God and the process." She blessed many by her life.

Joan and I started out living in a mobile home on her parents' farm. We welcomed people there, and I travelled from there giving workshops and retreats along with facilitating community renewal for religious congregations. But I had a little car, which in the winter often got stuck in the quarter of a mile driveway. One day I got stuck, kicked a tire, and said to God, "Enough already! We need a house, I don't care where it is, but it has to be fully furnished and free, because we weren't earning enough money to pay rent."

As it happened, the year before, Joan and I had gone to Pecos, New Mexico for a retreat with Morton Kelsey. We'd met three couples from Winnipeg there, along with their parish priest. Following the retreat, I began to do some formation with the couples, who added more couples to their group.

One day following my to-do with God, there was a call from the parish priest saying that the couple's group had a house for us if we would like it. The family that owned the house wanted to move to their country home to see how it fit them, so we would be able to have the house for about three years. It was fully furnished down to tea towels, and the couples who got together would rent it for our use. It really was the beginning of Joan's and my ministry together.

Following the three years, we bought a house from Homes for Growth, who were part of our own formation. They let us buy the house, paying what we could each month till it was paid off. I feel deeply humbled writing all this—so much grace, so much generosity, none of it deserved, all of it gift.

In the weeks and months of Joan's last year, the couples gathered each Monday after their work to pray with her. For years, people of the God With Us community—which Joan and I had established—gathered for Thursday evening prayer. In Joan's last year, people continued to gather without Joan being present. She remained in bed in her room while we prayed for her. Those who wished left her notes in a gathering book, journeying with her sight unseen.

Some weeks before her death, a couple came to visit. The young woman was someone Joan had accompanied in her spiritual journey over a few years. The young couple came and asked Joan—from her hospital bed at home—for a blessing. The young woman said, "Sister Joan, we have come to ask you to bless our child in my womb with your holy presence."

The dying journey is filled with sacredness. I was very privileged to be part of that journey. I would like to add here, that her physical journey was at times excruciating in its pain. She used to set a timer with a light so that she would take her pain medication every four hours. I began to administer her medication in the last two weeks or so of her life. Her doctor did house visits, and together they planned her pain management. Then when they had met, they brought me in to fill me in on what I could contribute to the process. As her dying time drew nearer, I asked who she would like to have with her in her last hours. She said, "You will know." And I did. I called her mother, her sister Theresa, and her friend Claire. For that final night, they were there. Her doctor wasn't available; he was delivering a baby.

And so again, how to open the well of absence? How to open and unveil months of intense presence and caring so the learnings can be gathered, and the grace given again and again can continue its offering for insight, wisdom, and personal gathering. Absence isn't empty space. It isn't a hole in need of filling. Rather, it is a holy space filled with grace. It offers a time to gather memories, regrets, what was lived well, what wasn't, so that it can teach and invite to a deeper integration and transformation.

Absence offers a time to grieve, to miss what was, what never came to be, what was lost. I am grateful for Jeanne, my spiritual accompanier, who so often listened and received this time of process and regathering. In the months following Joan's death, as I moved around in absence, I grappled with aloneness. In the course of Joan's dying time, I had emptied myself in order to be available, and now I had to find myself again.

I had images of a small figure on the other side of a ravine, a wide ravine, and as I prayed, the image would surface, and I would spend time looking at it, waiting for that part of me to come back to the rest of me, whatever that meant and was.

Absence is not an empty space; it is a consequence. Absence doesn't create itself; it is given in loss and carries an invitation for an expansion of the heart as a gathering place so that nothing once given is lost. It is a place where life lived is integrated at a new level, and what was fashioned in and through grace finds a new direction for offering.

*The future runs toward us, offering, inviting, stirring creativity to be activated through which the learnings gleaned can be nourishment for our choices, for not only our own future but for those who come after us. Living in Sacred Mystery, living in God, nothing is inconsequential, it all fashions us in some way, ultimately desiring to lead to the birthing of soul and discovery of our deepest freedom.*

– December 3, 1992

I have come to understand that dying is a very alone journey, no matter how close people are to us. People can be there to assure us, weep with us, hold us. But it's a journey only we can take. It's the aloneness we find ourselves held by at the point of birth, and the one that carries us through our lives. This aloneness is the ultimate point of our uniqueness within the creation of God. And it is facing that again and again, because it also carries our most unique gift to the world.

The hollowing-out of my heart by grief called me to step firmly into life so that nothing was lost. The naming of my process carried the grace to own what I lived and recognize the temptation to abdicate living for simple existence.

*If my garden offers me flowers every day*
*should I not go out and smell them and enjoy their beauty?*
*If a tree offers me shade from the blazing sun*
*should I not sit in its shadow and enjoy the sunlight?*
*If a bird offers me a song,*
*should I not pause and be filled by it?*
*And so, too, if my heart is given to love in abundance and*
*without condition*
*should I not respond and be glad?*

– May 1991

I found as I lived my process that there are different stages and levels to the process of grieving. I woke one morning and realized I had crossed a threshold. That small part of me across the ravine had come home. I felt a new clarity in me, and the space around me felt different as well. The next questions I was invited to consider were "What does this space around me mean, and what am I meant to follow in this inner clarity, what direction can I allow to surface?"

The first year brought an innumerable number of "if onlys": If only I had done, had known, would have been stronger, more caring and loving. Again, and again, I had to ground myself in the truth that I had done all that I could do, gave all that I had, and didn't know then what I know now. Following this process again and again, journaling again and again, fine tuning my inner ear to recognize and see the blessing, I began to name a remarkable learning. My "if onlys" were an entanglement of guilt and regret—regret carrying a deep sadness, and the guilt a merciless judge. I began to peel away the guilt from the regret and found through the regret a new aspect of the soul and person of the woman I had worked and lived with for so many years. We had been a great team, and our differences had also been great, sometimes separating us while moving us to simple acceptance of one another—though not without struggle and pain.

I still reverberate with the confrontation of love, when Jeanne, Clare, Raymond, and Joan gathered to challenge me to look into the eyes of love, the love that each of these people offered, seeing me and knowing me. That day the place of self-hatred, of despicableness, turned around and received and rested in beauty, in goodness, in mystery. The exit door, the escape route in me closed. I knew that I would need to learn to be with others in new ways, even though I was still most comfortable alone. The only one I had ever been most comfortable with was God. Before God, I was always fine. Before others, I was always challenged to live enough-ness. We need some form of community, some depth of relationship to be transformed in, and purified by. I have been fashioned to be a monastic, a contemplative. My prayer life, my solitude, grounds me in a consciousness, an awareness that is essential for the journey. But my wounded history, too, called me into integration and healing, again and again through relationship, friendship, and community, working and living with others. To become fully human, fully who we are at the heart of us, is our journey. It is this process of emergence in and through relationship that unveils our goodness and our holiness and calls forth our essential purpose. As my fourth-grade teacher said to me so many years ago: "Each of you are created for a special purpose". So....

In closing part one of this book, I invite you to become who you are. In that is grace and blessing

*We are made for ecstasy, not despair . . . fullness of life, not death; love, not isolation.*
*The question again becomes: how to teach what I have been given to know and understand?*
*How to invite the unshuttering of minds and hearts*
*so that each one would desire to find their own inner way?*
*How to have the process of my own life transformed, broken, and given as bread of life?*

*– May 1995*

# PART TWO

—

# The Sacred Call

*Morning came and evening came.*
*And on the evening that I was born,*
*God looked at me with love, tenderness,*
*and compassion and said that I was good.*

*Then this Sacred Mystery offered me to the world to become how I*
*was given,*
*a presence of love, a gift of grace, and a member of all that is family*
*in creation.*
*It meant birth, death, resurrection, again and again.*
*Falling and rising, practicing the invitation*
*into the incarnate reality of Love over and over,*
*knowing that this pilgrimage of Sacred Becoming*
*was both an invitation and a mandate.*
*All of creation is a sacred experiment*
*of unveiling the deep and unfathomable love*
*out of which we have come.*
*And so, this journey.*

*– October 1993*

Over the many years of my life, I have focused on the interior development of people, the liberation and the naming of their inner selves, the reordering of beliefs and values so that the whole person, that which is their essential self, their best self, can emerge. Being awake, being conscious, being available to the unveiling of life, of invitation, of sacredness, is ultimately the grace of being a human being, born into consciousness. Entry into relationship with the whole of creation, the universe, the Sacred Energy that we breathe in, and which breathes in us, we become one with all that is. This is not a journey to be taken alone. This is a time for accompaniment, for friendship, for reflection and contemplation, for community, for the companionship of empowerment, following the movements of the heart and the spirit, so that nothing is lost, and the dreaming within creation can reach its fullness.

*What is required of me is:*
*to be vigilant,*
*to be attentive,*
*to face fully who and what I am,*

*what I carry,*
*own my history without being bound by it.*
*Sacred Presence, Holy Wisdom has always sat at the edge of my*
*soul, available.*
*Grace abounds.*
*Truth frees.*
*I have the courage necessary.*
*I place myself in Wisdom's hands.*
*I listen faithfully to the invitation in Sacred time.*
*Fidelity renders me obedient to the Sacred Mystery and the*
*Sacred Way.*

*– June 18, 1993*

# CHAPTER 15:
# Paths of Integration

## *Developing a Disposition to Grace*

This intimate journey of integration requires that we open ourselves to an awareness of our various dispositions. An important starting point for me is the disposition to Grace, that radiant energy in the universe that requires an interior attitude of humility and availability. That is, accepting myself as I am, no more and no less. It means availing the inner listener in me to see, hear, and understand beyond what seems reasonable. It requires the ancient stance of being in the presence of the Holy One, both in the within and the beyond of me, and standing in stillness before God, so that Holy Wisdom can be the action. This carries the attitude and disposition of abandonment, to receive wisdom and direction in front of what is before me so that the choices and responses I make are in keeping with my journey to wholeness and holiness.

As a result of my God seizure so many years earlier, when I was at the edge of being thirty, I have learned to lean into the humanity of Jesus. Becoming familiar with Jesus as brother, as friend and companion, as path maker and as status quo breaker, has allowed me to take liberties with some of his story. I don't mean that I change the scriptures, but I play, and interpret some pieces that simplify my perspective of this incredible teacher who unveils the face and heart of God. It is how I tell Jesus stories to children, and to whoever has an open heart to be moved into their own innocence to hear the word of the God of love and keep it.

Leaning into the life of Jesus early in my life helped me develop what I call my "rule of life." It is simple, really, but it is also challenging. This simple little rule of life has managed to travel to different parts of the world and change many lives. It continues to fashion mine. I will share it shortly. But first, let me take you into my imaginary telling of one Jesus story.

## *Unravelling to the Sacred Impulse*

This story carries the power of water. It also carries an invitation for our own journey as Christians. Perhaps you might consider reading it out loud and hearing it read to your inner self so that you, too, hear yourself named.

Once there was a boy named Jesus. He was taught well in the old ways. Each day he rose in prayer and praised God, "Blessed be God's name." He grew strong in his faith and his awareness, which was honed by his mother, Mary, and his father, Joseph.

He was raised in a society where 98 percent of the people were poor. They were highly taxed by the Herodian rulers who collected taxes and turned these over to the Roman government. They also paid additional taxes to the temple in which he prayed. It was difficult for people to live. Jesus grew into a man quietly. He learned his father Joseph's trade, and his father and mother witnessed to him the faith of his ancestors, the teachings of the prophets, and the law of God.

Then one day he reconnected with his cousin, John, who was said to have been in the desert for years, being taught by a hermit. John had come to speak of conversion and repentance, calling people to a change of heart, to a deep understanding of the ways of the world and the longing of God. Jesus heard, knew, and understood, and his own Dream of God stirred within him. He was grateful for John.

Through their conversations, John came to recognize Jesus as a Holy One of God. He began to point to him, make others aware of him. Jesus was of humble heart and didn't really intend to be in the limelight. Then one day, while John was baptising in the Jordan, he decided to enter the waters himself, and so began his own journey with those who had taken the plunge. As Jesus entered the waters, the heavens opened and the Great Spirit, the Kiss from the Mouth of God, rested on him and said, "You are my beloved son, in you I am well pleased."

That day, Jesus was seized by the dream and passion of God and went into the desert to grapple with this dream and passion of God that had awakened in him. And so—to our awareness—began his journey of subversion, of being countercultural, of being obedient to his inner promptings toward the revelation of God's dream written within him.

In this grappling, he was tempted with the economic power of the world, and he said, "No, I choose the poor."

He was tempted with the security and comfort of kinship, of patriarchy; he said, "No. I choose all those who hear the word of God and keep it."

He was tempted with the safety of conventional wisdom, and he said, "No, I choose the way of compassion and mercy, so that all come to know, as I know, the God who is merciful and compassionate."

And so it was. Jesus began his journey of subversion by making forgiveness the grace of his baptism; by making compassion and mercy the central way of non-violence; and community the grace and blessing of love and transformation for all. These are central to his Sacred Impulse, as well as much of his teaching as a Jew among his own people. It is this Sacred Impulse that motivated the ethic by which he lived. Sometimes people speak of God's central character as "compassionate," and God's ethic as "justice," and the "right relationship." We all have the capacity for the awakening of the sacred impulse through which God, Holy Wisdom, comes to us. It is that which moves our passion toward life; it calls us to a deep obedience, a deep listening, and toward action that contributes to the emergence of life. It is a central energy of our soul, and the longing for wholeness in ourselves, in our relationships, and in our world. This is neither compulsive nor impulsive since these tend to feed the ego, or our unmet needs. The Sacred Impulse cannot compromise life. It does allow for concessions, because in this place we can discern big deals and little deals. It is this Sacred Impulse in Jesus that released God's radical love. And it is this uncompromising reality, this radical obedience to the unveiling of God's dream, that got Jesus executed.[7]

The above brush stroke is a synthesis of just one part of a big story. Holding this synthesis helped me climb more deeply into the humanity of Jesus and form what I call my "rule of life."

- I began by following Jesus around the scriptures. In my place of contemplation, I watched how Jesus listened to people, how he looked at people, how he touched people, took time with people, and when he went off to pray.
- Then I chose to let him look at me, especially in those times I was most deeply in need of healing, of being listened to, or needing to be embraced or taken time with or in those moments when I felt most alone.
- Then I chose to practice this look, exercise my listening heart, receive the grief and pain in need of an embrace, of a physical presence of silence.
- Then I chose to touch people as I experienced Jesus touch me with reverence and compassion, sometimes holding them as

---

7   Doreen Kostynuik: part of presentation to participants present at Faith and Sharing retreat August 2020.

they wept, taking their hand as they shared. Being a point of intercession in quiet prayer for their healing, their need of insight, or being gently present in the dying process.
- Then I chose to sit and rest in prayer, waiting for the Holy One to rest me and embolden me to live the mystery and presence of love and radical obedience.

This is a deeply formative process of the inner journey, and imperative work to unearth the Sacred Impulse that carries our essential action for partnership in the emergence of life. In his little book called *The Universe is a Green Dragon*, Brian Swimme says, "Be patient, for there is certainly specific work waiting for you. Or did you think that the universe went to twenty billion years of work to create you if there was not a particular function that you—and *only* you—could do? The creative powers residing in you will be evoked in time for the work they were created for."[8]

Following Jesus around the scriptures, learning from him the way of love, of mercy and compassion, continues to beckon me. Following Jesus around the scriptures while he welcomed those who were poor, those at the margins, those who sought justice continues to invite me. Following Jesus around the scriptures and watching him challenge or confront those who used power to diminish women, children, men who were stripped of their manhood when they could no longer work to feed their families, calls me to be aware of how I can put people in categories because of their addictions or weird behaviour. Following Jesus around the scriptures invites me to enter deeply into his humanity so that I can be led to the big God of the universe who is unveiled by the fullness of each blade of grass, each singing bird, and each person becoming fully who they are made to be, a revelation of the divine, an unveiling of the sacred that breathes and has its being in all that is for relationship. The incarnation is the self-revelation of the One who is in all that is held in Sacred Mystery, coming toward us from the future as an

---

8    Swimme, Brian, *The Universe is A Green Dragon: A Cosmic Creation Story,* ((Bear & Company, Inc.1984), 14-9.

invitation to continue cooperating with what is not-yet. There is a Hebrew word for that. Be Kadosh, be sacred beings![9]

My rule of life in summary:

> Follow Jesus around the scriptures.
> Watch how he moves among people, how he looks at them.
> Notice how he bends to touch, to welcome, to listen.
> Rest in what you have seen, observed, noticed.

Now:

> Let him look at you, let him see you, your goodness, your beauty; let him see what you are most reluctant to have anyone see: your weaknesses, what you reject and refuse to own in yourself, or what you hide from others. Notice how he looks at you with love and compassion, with tenderness and acceptance.
> Rest in what you have allowed to be seen, touched, held, and loved in you.

Then:

> Become the look.
> Become the touch.
> Become the listening heart and mind.
> Become the look that dares to see and know where wounds reside, where fear of rejection hides, become the look that takes into itself what needs to be reverenced, believed, seen, heard, understood.
> Rest in this reality of incarnation, be a bearer of compassion, of truth, of mercy. Let your love and attentiveness stand in stillness in the Wisdom of God and guide you breath by breath so that holy intention

---

9    Prager, Marcia Rabbi. *The Path of Blessings*: Experiencing the Energy and Abundance of the Divine. First Jewish Lights Quality Paperback Edition (Woodstock VT. Jewish Lights Publishing 2003), 10

can guide you and release within you your own Sacred Impulse.

## Consciousness, Wakefulness as Doorway

*Keep in mind:*
*The longness of life is shorter than the reality*
*Each day fades into the next like the rising and evaporation of mist.*
*So, embrace it deeply, and reverently.*
*Commit to life's challenges and invitation*
*so that nothing of it will be lost.*
*Ground yourself in your soul so that you*
*seek not relief from life, but the maturity to choose life.*
*Struggle, grow, give birth to life within you*
*and find there that all is sacred.*
*Let life take hold of you,*
*embrace you,*
*challenge you,*
*transform you,*
*lead you,*
*love you.*
*And know that life is ultimately not of your making.*
*Rather it is your response.*

*– June 1993*

Cosmic spirituality introduces us to the big bang theory that comes out of quantum physics. I like to refer to it as the sacred flare and continue to imagine the story where, out of nothing, life came. In this nothingness, there is an uncreated reality that carries a genius for creativity, a consciousness that creates relationship through the infusion of matter with itself. Following this emerging reality of the conscious-self of love, uniting atoms into life forms experimenting with possibility, I find myself living on a little blue dot in an ever-emerging cosmos. This cosmos invites me to become fully who I am, along with others, to fall in love with a dreaming God. All of life is infused with grace. The foundation of this grace is conscious-ness that moves and breathes and has its being in what is and what is not-yet.

In the prologue of John's gospel we read, "In the beginning was the word and the word was with God, and the word was God." And then in John's gospel Jesus says, "You will not only do what I have done but greater things than these."

If in fact we are empowered to be as Jesus was—to do all that he did and even greater things because of his fidelity and uncom-promising love of God, as well as his immersion in the Sacred Consciousness—what is required of us to be as he was? How do we go to the end of our love? What form of disposition is required for this giving and gift of life lived? If, for example, I dispose myself to listening, I must empty myself to the interior silence of the heart so that I can hear beyond words and see beyond expressions. When I listen to women in recovery from addiction, sharing with me their fifth step[10], I must be free from the clutter of assumptions and judge-ments so that my heart can be a place where life can be washed in love and acceptance: My eyes rooted in this love, my face reflecting the acceptance and love of who they are as they share and claim and own their personal journey. Sometimes the pain of their lives is so big for them that they must have another's heart available to hold them while they share—because they could have died and didn't. They bring themselves into this moment, they sit humbly in front of me bringing me their story, and I, in turn, am humbled by the privilege of their trust and courage. This depth of listening is not an intellectual exercise, it is the exercise of grace in Sacred Presence. It is in this Sacred Presence that we find and meet Christ-Sophia, Jesus-Sophia,[11] the Wisdom within all of creation.

---

10   The Fifth Step in the Recovery Program asks that the addict admit to God, or to a Higher Power, to themselves, and to another human being the exact nature of their wrong.

11   Johnson, Elizabeth A. She Who Is: The Mystery of God in Feminist Theological Discourse, (The Crossroad Publishing Company 1992) throughout book.

Living Sacred Consciousness is resting in the gentle, wakeful-ness of Sacred Presence. It is an energy that moves within the whole universe, that nudges us to be aware of what is around us, to what is before us, and to what is within us. Sacred Consciousness moves in every cell of our body. The body is responsive to the energy that moves in a room, to the wind, the trees. It's available to hold within it what is dealt with and what waits to be received, unshuttered, that can lead to our own deepest freedom. The body can release what Sacred Consciousness would like to free in us. Sacred Consciousness is really an invitation within creation to become itself. Creation becomes itself through awareness. Our awareness contributes to that coming to be.

Sacred Consciousness is the creativity of divine nature. We come out of that consciousness as human beings, as does the tree, as does the bird. Sacred Consciousness releases creativity because it lives response to the invitation of the future imagining itself into being. In every moment the future runs toward us full of invitation. As I have continued to reflect on Sophia Wisdom, today as I continue to become aware of her as indwelling, teaching, leading, holding, abiding, accompanying, "meeting me in every thought"[12], today in my prayer, I became aware of the more. If I can reflect on the vast-ness of the cosmic universe, is not the inner universe also vast and spacious, filled with emerging mystery to be unveiled and explored and lived as conscious gift as revelation within relationship? And does not this unveiling actually come through contemplation, through uncluttering and healing, through owning our history and being present in this moment toward all moments?

So today, as we bend into our lives: What forms us, in-forms us? How does the movement of our own Sacred Impulse infused with the possible, held by the heart of creation, whisper gently, availing us to the best of who we are in our humanity?

Today, in this time of our life, what names us, sends us forth, invites us, unveils our desires, dreams, through which events, which relationships? Being available, willing to be learners, moving into

12   Wisdom 6:16

the realm of transforming grace and bending into the opening up of our lived experience, perhaps we can come to realize that all of who we are and move in is relationship. We are part of a vast reality of wholeness in emerging grace. What are some of the necessary ingredients, the essential elements?

As infants we start by taking everything in without discernment. We tend to believe what we see and hear and build our world view on this intake. Children are generally very good perceivers and poor interpreters. That's why they need adults to guide and clarify what is perceived, so that they can build their self-trust. This helps us as we mature, to learn to process and activate our own ability to discern and make choices that are helpful to our wellbeing. So, self-reflection and life-giving relationships are essential.

Living in Sacred Consciousness sometimes comes through a shattering experience, one that empties us and confronts us and faces us with choosing to explore the devastation, to run for the hills and bury ourselves in work, isolation, depression, or to some form of addiction or escape.

In order to move toward conversion, activate our inner self-conversation for the purpose of understanding what is inside a feeling or reaction, we need to meet ourselves in our unfinishedness, and open up our intentions, both conscious and unconscious. This involves moving away from the inner critic or the judge that often follows us around, or the ego that justifies or rationalizes, or moves toward blaming another or a situation or event, or that builds escape routes from unpacking what has happened. That doesn't mean we are responsible for everything because that is not true. It is being able to have some level of understanding to generate options, choices for how to live from the best in us, and what to do with what we unpack in our findings.

There are times when we do miss the mark, where we have a divided heart, or are living from a divided heart, where we have or are contributing to division through superiority, competition, or self-hatred and self-rejection. Conversion implies having conversation with how we live our lives on a daily basis. It implies reflecting

**DOREEN D. KOSTYNUIK**

on our lived experience, examining what situations require mutuality, equality, compassion, mercy, justice, and right relations, and seeing how and what we contribute to the moment. Conversion implies a change of mind, of seeing things more clearly, more deeply, that moves us to insight, and to a point of decision, to then act on what we have come to know, see, and understand. That is what leads to transformation. Transformation is embodying the insight or understandings given through our reflection and change of mind. It carries not only intentionality but decisiveness. Now this is not about the will power of the ego, but an act of will to be exercised according to the heart. The heart, the place of our deepest freedom, is the seat of wisdom.

Our will is meant to be placed at the service of the seeing and knowing of the heart. We have been taught to use willpower so as to always be in control. This keeps us in our heads and in a fragile ego that uses language like this: "I will force myself to do this or that, or I will try to make you do this or that." The fragile ego mistakes power for strength, always needs to be right, tends to be judgmental and driven. The ego is principled but not always intelligent. It has limited understanding, and can be governed by "shoulds," "oughts," and "have-to's." In this reality, it is not connected to the desire of inner freedom. The ego is meant to be at the service of the heart, at the service of inner wisdom, otherwise it is simply a control freak. On its own, it pushes our desire, our hopes, into ambition. It carries a measuring stick, compares us not for learning but for judgement, because someone has to be up or down. This seeking to be holy, then, is not about wholeness, compassion, mercy, and right relationships, but about perfection, flawlessness, about rules and regulations that have to be followed with rigidity. It is outside-in living and not grounded in the soul. It is about being seen and it engenders fear of being wrong. It carries a driver, not a responder to what is required, or necessary, for life in the moment. As we become more conscious and develop our inner listening, then the will is used to follow an insight. When it chooses to accept what is found, and follows the desire of the heart, the inclination of the inner self that carries the

110

longing for wholeness, the will is no longer ego-based but aligned with the desire of inner wisdom, the fullness of our humanity.

Now, choosing to follow this inner invitation doesn't mean it always feels great. Sometimes there is resistance to follow, but underneath the resistance is a knowing that this is the way I must follow. It is an interior mandate connected to life. And it is here that I bend into my rule of life, following what I have learned from Jesus about being faithful in all things and in all ways. This practice and discipline continues to be given to me through my prayer and reflection to guide my journey.

# CHAPTER 16:
## Forgiveness

## *Forgiveness: Part One*

For me, forgiveness has been a big process of learning. It's not to forgive and forget, confess my sins, and get on with life. I have learned this form of confession, this relief of guilt—without a change of mind and heart that leads to new learning—simply gives me permission to repeat the behaviour or attitude, because I paid the price by feeling so badly. Nor is forgiveness shoving down the hurt and covering it over with a brave face and pretending all is fine. Nor is it talking about the event or hurt ad nauseum, recycling over and over, hoping it will all go away, hoping judgement of the "other" will be made and you will have had your revenge. Forgiveness is a process. Forgiveness, often when connected to serious realities, carries grief that needs to be dealt with because it involves levels of loss. And there are some realities that are unforgiveable. There are realities that cannot be resolved. And we have to decide how to be in front of them, what to do with them. Forgiveness involves a process that in some cases is quite simple and other times requires work and time. Talking to a listener who receives and, when appropriate, gives feedback, journaling, and reaching into the best in us that allows us to journey and be a life learner—these are some ways that are available to us to embrace this invitation, to stand fully in ourselves, to live from our deepest freedom. In our deepest freedom, our inner guide resides, Sacred Wisdom waits, and we are taught to be bearers of grace because we contribute to the life coming to itself in new ways. Forgiveness ultimately frees us.

Now, in life there are big deals and little deals. The undealt-with little deals can accumulate and pile up and then be weaponised. So, in my house, where I share and live community with Mary, I have asked that she and I deal with issues as they come up so that we live with as much clarity as we can. I also ask that of my friends. Those who know me know I have a strong personality, and in spite of my gentleness, I am also bossy. I can say things too strongly and be offensive. Many times, I become conscious of my tone of voice or actions after the fact and then ask for forgiveness. I learned many years ago that when I said I was sorry, others would say, "Don't worry about it," or, "It's okay." And I would think, *If it was okay, I wouldn't be feeling badly*—because my conscience said I missed the mark, I wasn't being aware of the other, and what I needed to hear is that am I forgiven. We practice forgiveness often in our house, learning over and over to be faithful to who we are in relationship to the other.

A small example: Mary and I live in community and have established a house of welcome. People come for rest, for spiritual direction or therapy, for retreat, or just to have conversation, to share a meal, and to share life. We like to grow our own vegetables and have built some raised beds. Two summers ago, we decided to add two new raised garden beds, one that was two-by-six, and another for a young, ten-year-old friend that was two-by-four. We bought boards and corners. I have a mitre saw so cut the boards to length, and we began. It is very simple, really, except Mary and I talk about the same thing differently, and we get frustrated with each other because we don't know what the other really means. Finally, we get it, she will say something, and I will say, "Well, that's what I was saying." And we get on with it.

Now there is no sin here, but frustration doesn't render me patient, and it challenges my tolerance for difference. So, at the end of the day, when I gather my gratitudes, I also ask forgiveness for my impatience. And I hear "you're forgiven." "You are forgiven" is a powerful phrase. I have seen people's whole bodies shift into an ease when they feel they have blown it and hear they are forgiven and get another chance. I like the invitation from the gospel that asks me to be faithful in little things so that I know what it means to be faithful in big ones.

As I said earlier, we have to educate our sensitivity. We can so easily use it against ourselves and feel guilty about "spilt milk," or we can be mindful and learn to live community, friendship, with ease. Now, be careful, I am not talking about scrupulosity. Scrupulosity is developed by the ego, has measuring sticks, perfectionistic tendencies, is fear-laden. Mindfulness in relationship is shaped by kindness and a listening heart. Mindfulness also carries the invitation to explore the purpose reflected in behaviour, and the desire to understand the motivation and the underlying need expressed in it.

In the early '70s I was an elementary school counsellor for the Edmonton Catholic School System. I worked between two schools in the inner city. One day, I received a call from the local police department telling me about a little boy in first grade who was caught lighting garage fires in the back lane, and asking if I could "fix him." "I don't think I can fix him," I said, "but I would be very happy to see him."

I asked the boy's teacher to send him to my office. When he arrived, he opened the mail slot in my office door, which happened to be the right height for him to bend into, and yelled, "Hello, I'm here!"

I responded, "Come on in." I was sitting in a low-level chair because I like to meet children at eye level.

He came in, wandered around my office, looking at the plants, picking up little fuzzy things on the shelf beside me, stopping by the pencil sharpener to try to read the little sign below it: *Don't try to understand me, just love me.* He stopped, turned to me, and said, "Well, what do you want?"

I was still pretty new to the school and didn't have anything on my walls, so I said to him, "Sammie, I am in my office a lot; I don't have anything on my walls, and I wonder if you could draw me something and come and visit me and have a conversation."

He looked at me awhile. Then he said, "Okay."

We began our journey together. He was a little boy whose mother was an alcoholic, a little boy who made his mother breakfast and often missed school or got there late, a little boy whose father worked in the north and was home intermittently. He was a little boy who needed attention, care, to be seen and encouraged to see himself as capable, as good. One of the things I knew and taught at the time is that misbehaving children are discouraged children. Part of my work was to find ways to understand what the child is saying and seeking through his behaviour and then empower the teacher and the child to help find his inner courage, so that he could learn to make decisions and take responsibility for his choices. I visited his classroom, had conversations with the teacher, and one day asked if she could have a job for him that only he would do.

She said, "But what about the other children? How can I single him out?"

"Do the other children need what he does at this time?"

"Not exactly," she said.

So, she brought a plant into the classroom that he was in charge of watering, which he did very faithfully.

It was a process. One day he arrived at my office with his whole face dirty except for the tip of his nose. Somewhere he'd leaned against a window to try to see inside.

I looked at him, and I said, touching the tip of my own nose, "Sammie, I can see this much of your face."

He began to rub his face and asked if I would like to see the rest of it.

I said yes. I just happened to have a supplied bathroom in my office, with a little stool. He went into the bathroom, scrubbed his face clean, then came out and showed it to me. I took his little face into my hands, looked all over it, and said, "What a beautiful face you have, Sammie. I am so glad to see it!"

Ever after, a little face would show up at my office to be gazed at and delighted in.

My office walls became gradually covered in large drawings of people being shot down out of open windows in skyscrapers—until one day, finally, a little boy in a giant snowmobile emerged in Sammie's artwork, as he began to find a sense of a self.

By this time, we were moving into the Christmas break. Over these initial months, there were frequent calls through the mail slot in my office door announcing, "I'm here!" and I would have to go to the door and say that I was with someone and would see him later. I discovered, at one point, that his teacher thought he was making bathroom stops when he came to see me.

On one of the last days before Christmas break, he made his office stop, came in to tell me more of his story, that his dad was coming home. As he was leaving, I asked if I got a Merry Christmas hug.

He looked at me and said, "No way."

I smiled and said, "Okay have a good Christmas."

He made for the door, stopped, turned, and said in a big voice, "Oh, all right!" Then he came back and hugged me in my low-to-the-ground chair. He put his little arms around my neck and hugged me tighter and tighter, and as he let go, he said. "Goodbye, auntie," and left.

The next morning, I was to be at my other school and had forgotten something in my office that I needed. I came into the school and recognized a little body coming in the door at the other end of the hall. I stopped as I recognized Sammie. He saw me and ran toward me. When he was near enough, he fell against the wall, and collapsed to the floor. I knew it was all for my benefit, so that I would notice him and respond to him. I smiled at him, and dropped to my knees in front of him and asked, "Sammie, do you need a hug?" He said yes and came into my arms and rested there a while before I left. At the end of the school year, Sammie was going to be moving and couldn't take the plant he was caring for with him, so the teacher invited him to come and plant it in her garden. She promised to care for it for him.

How do I read the purpose, motivation, need, in a child's behaviour? For Sammie, I knew it was a need for my attention. It was the only way he knew how to ask. If I have an understanding of the behaviour, how do I respond to the need that is underneath the behaviour so that in the case of misbehaviour I don't feed the misbehaviour and find a way to respond to the need? It takes attentiveness and practice. As an educator I often asked: How do I help this child belong, be seen, be accepted so that he can grow into a relationship of equals, able to contribute, stand in his own strength as a becoming person? I once heard Rudolph Dreikurs say (on tape), "To understand a child's behaviour, you need to watch where her feet point." And another phrase: "Learn to take your sail out of his wind," so that you don't get into a power struggle, feeding the unquenchable need for attention, what I call the hole in the heart, or the "I can't" syndrome that says, "I couldn't yesterday, and I can't today and don't even think things will change tomorrow," which pulls us into the game of rescuing. Try to see what's underneath what is in front of you, what is the perceived need. If it's attention, give it when she is not asking, if it's power, side-step it and find a way in by another door. Learn to listen inside the movement and respond to what is needed not demanded. And in this learning learn to listen inside of your/our own reactions, learn to hold softly your inner pain, come to see and hear and work to understand what your motivation is as well, as your intention in some of your interactions, what was hoped for and missed, what was given and not received. Take the sail out of your turbulent reaction so that you can come to know and understand what moves in you more deeply. In this way you can follow the process of your inner life to forgiveness, learn to let go in grief, and move toward understanding what we need to be reconciled with.

This process of learning is one of the reasons I respect so much the commitment lived by the women at Talitha Koum Houses, where they are supported in a recovery journey from abuse, addictions, and loss of their children. They not only share their journey, but at the end of my time of listening, their journey calls me to continue my own self-examination. What these women share in working their fourth and fifth steps is their process of making amends, of dealing with their resentments, their wounded histories of abuse. For some, this is what led them to prison or the loss of their children, and their desire for freedom and wholeness. For them to make amends, they are invited to come to terms with their part in hurting others and being unfaithful to their own lives. They look at their resentments, their expectations of others and themselves, and how others' failures to meet their needs led them to their choices. They must become reconciled with what they cannot change in order to free themselves of the memories that hold them in bondage. They must embrace what has marked them, befriend what triggers their unhealthy reactions, know what awakens their defence system, so that they can accept their history and choose life with reframed patterns.

Learning to forgive is a process. Learning to forgive is different from reconciliation. They are two paths that intertwine, that are woven into an inner fabric of learning toward inner freedom. Forgiveness is not an act of will. Rather it is the desire of our deepest freedom, the seat of Wisdom herself that helps us navigate toward reconciliation of what is unfinished and what must be let go of so that we are free.

Four faces of reconciliation:
- I need to be reconciled with reality. What is this reality before me that I need to walk through to understand to the best of my ability? How do I stand before it to get perspective? What am I powerless to change or resolve? It is what it is. I may hate

it, be saddened by it, angered by it, but none of that frees me to embrace the future.

- I need to be reconciled with God. What is it that I wanted God to do or be that God wasn't? What image of God do I carry? Is God like Santa Claus, a policeman, a magician, a stern judge, a God of distant places who simply observes and is disengaged from my reality? Is God a Sacred Presence intimately engaged in my life, accompanying me, weeping with me, encouraging me every breath of my way? Who and how is this God living and breathing in my life, my awareness, my consciousness? What for me is God's job?
- I need to be reconciled with others. Who are they for me? What have been my expectations of them, my need of them? What are my disappointments in relation to them? What can I let go of, accept, or let be? Is it time to walk away? If so, what do I leave behind?
- I need to be reconciled with myself. What might I have done differently if anything? What was I powerless to change, do, or be? What follows me around that I carry and need to let go of, trusting I did the best I knew to do in that moment? Can I allow myself to be a person in process, choosing life again and again?

In all of this, what is important for me is to remain attentive to what has no resolution so that we don't try to fix the unfixable or forgive the unforgivable. Putin invading Ukraine is unforgivable. Human trafficking of women and children is unforgivable. Rape is unforgivable, and the list can go on.

## Forgiveness: Part Two

Before moving into the coming process, I want to introduce you to the Poustinik reality in me, give a preamble, and speak of my hermitage, because it is there that I prayed, grappled, and integrated some essential pieces of my life toward liberation. A Poustinik is an ancient Byzantine term for one who goes into solitude for others.

In 1984, Joan and I moved into a house on Muriel Street in Winnipeg. We bought that house with a small down payment and paid what we could each month till it was paid off. There was no bank mortgage, just a commitment, a contract. If we couldn't finish paying for it, we would return it. (At the end, when the title was transferred, the lawyer was disbelieving that no bank was involved, no lawyer or notary witnessing it, only our word and our integrity in commitment.)

One of the first things I chose to do when moving into the house was build a hermitage in half of the garage so that I could spend time in solitude (usually one full day a week and later each morning, for periods of time). It is where I continued to follow my inner work, it is where I mounted icons that I had photographed because I hadn't taken any training yet to write my own; icons for the Byzantines are written and meant to be read, rather than painted and looked at. In most Ukrainian homes, you find an icon mounted on a wall or on a table, always reminding us to remain in the presence of the sacred. And in the "reading" of the icon, we practice the prayer of gazing. And it is in the hermitage that I am given what to hold in praying for others around me and in the world. I have learned to put my head in my heart and stand in stillness before God so God can direct my action. I have learned to filter the pain and suffering others live without absorbing it and making it my own.

I once heard Ron Rolheiser say, speaking about the crucifixion, that Jesus stretched out his arms on the cross, took in the anger and hatred into himself and poured out love. For me, the reality of the Eucharist, the binding of Oneness empowers me to do that. I also use the Jesus prayer, an ancient prayer at the heart in the Eastern church, that stills my heart and my life. The Jesus prayer is a breath prayer, breathing in the consciousness of Jesus, the reality of Jesus, and letting go into the graciousness of God when breathing out. It is a prayer that has saved me when driving through snowstorms, when sitting at the side of the sick or dying. It is a prayer that leads me to sleep, it is the prayer I use in powerlessness and helplessness, and sometimes I simply use the name of Jesus when I'm looking for a parking spot, especially when I am in a hurry.

Catherine Doherty, the founder of the Combermere community, is someone I met in my twenties, who invited me to be a Poustinik in the marketplace: to be a presence of prayer wherever I went. I have not forgotten the invitation.

In 1974-75, I began facilitating days of reflection for groups in hospitals or parishes outside of my teaching counselling work for the school system. And then in 1975, I took a year's leave of absence from the school system to discern what I wanted to do with the rest of my life, one possibility being entering a religious community again. That summer, I was asked to facilitate a one-week process to two groups of a Ukrainian order of religious women. That was such a gift for me. In the first session, when I stood in front of all these women, I found myself filled with emotion because as I looked out at them, I recognized myself, I touched into my own spirit as a Byzantine. That summer work led me to work with a number of religious congregations around the country. It amazed me that something that I carried could encourage and nourish as it did. I was also amazed to learn which people I turned off, and how. This, too, is invitation to integration and humility. The gift and grace of that year led me to choose this work as part of my inner mandate to service. My spiritual director at the time, a Sister of Holy Cross, helped me understand that I was meant for religious life, without necessarily being in a congregation. She suggested that I might be freer to do more outside than inside. True or not, I know that I have not regretted following this inner path; God has been very faithful to me, and I have found life, joy, and continued wonder everywhere I have gone with and through nearly everyone I have met.

One of the groups I worked with over an extended period of time brought me to one of my deepest learnings about forgiveness, reconciliation, and holy detachment. Holy detachment allows me to hold what is before me with softness, resting and living from my deepest freedom. There was at one time a major bump, a big misunderstanding that I didn't know how to get through except do my inner work—lots of journaling, solitude, spiritual accompaniment, and prayer. Now, the misunderstanding wasn't with the whole community; it was with Margaret Anne who was the person in leadership, but it felt like the whole community in me. I had chosen to support a decision one of her members had taken that was contrary to her belief system. I thought that she was more open and had more inner space to hold what her member found she had to live. I never thought that the decision taken would be used against me. I felt deeply hurt because I had come to know, love, and respect this person and her community. I felt with all the time we spent working together that Margaret Anne knew me and believed in the work I did with her members. In retrospect, I believe that she followed her own conscience, her own perception and interpretation of the decision I made. And that was her job, her responsibility. At that point, my responsibility was to deal with my own lack of understanding and hurt. And this is the journey I want to open up to you, with the hopes it helps you in your own journey to liberation and abiding in grace.

Apart from journaling, talking through some of this, and getting through my stunned inner silence, I began to make a list of all the positive I knew and believed about this woman and made it a litany in my morning or evening prayer. I needed to create some inner distance so that I didn't become cynical or negative because that would just erode my heart. I wasn't always gracious, with feelings and judgments bumping into each other, but I had to find a way through. I had the power to choose this journey, even kicking and screaming at times. Bitterness was not an option I wanted to entertain. The other thing I knew was that because I travelled the country and so did she, I could one day bump into her in an airport. And in fact, this did occur one day: I was sitting between flights in a small airport, and there she was coming down the escalator. So, what were my three choices? Either/or isn't a choice so I had to generate three.

1. I could sit where I was and ignore her, pretend I didn't notice her as she passed by the area that I was in.
2. I could leave and go to another area of the airport.

Or:

3. I could acknowledge her without any obligation on my part or hers to engage. A nod of acknowledgement on my part would do. So, I asked myself a question: "Doreen, what is your nature? In any other circumstance what would you do?" I would acknowledge her. So, I looked up as she passed and nodded. She responded with a nod.

I also drove between provinces in those days, and in the old days I would have stopped in the small town where the congregation had a house for a cup of tea. The first six months of driving through the town, I asked myself, "Do I have enough strength to stop today?" I would check into my inner self, and if I didn't, I would keep driving. One day I was driving through, asked the question as I always did, and I had enough strength to stop, knock on the door and simply say hello. A few months later I had enough strength to stop in for five minutes. And so it went until I could manage a cup of tea and be present in my freedom to whoever was in front of me. And at no time did we get into what had happened, because even though the women were aware that something had happened, it was not a topic for general conversation.

However, at some point in the following years, I made a retreat with the Lynn brothers who at that time were Jesuits, and a few members of Margaret Anne's community were present. One of the rituals we were invited to was the washing of feet. I approached one of the members of the community, and in love and kindness, we washed each other's feet as a sign of forgiveness in the mystery that lay between us.

The impasse I lived with in the face of her leadership was not about her; I had to continue my inner work so that I lived free and continued to choose life and be faithful in all things and in all ways. That was my responsibility. Throughout all of this process, the Jesus prayer was on my lips and in my heart. One of the gifts and graces of the Jesus prayer is that when we pray it long enough and deeply enough, it begins to pray itself within us. The interpretation that I use is: "Jesus, Beloved One, son of God, son of Mary, have mercy." I use a set of one hundred beads that I pray slowly, breathing in and letting go into God. If I am driving, I sing it. It is always in the presence of mercy and loving kindness. Thomas Hopko, in his book *The Lenten Spring,* speaks of mercy, using the Hebrew translation for *hesed,* which he says can be translated into English in many different ways. He says:

> Some bibles say mercy, others say steadfast love, while still others say tenderness or loving kindness or simply love. So, it may as well be translated as 'Lord, be merciful, gracious, kind, generous, compassionate, bountiful, loving.' According to God's self-revelation, God is all of these things, whether we pray to God or not. So, when we pray, Lord have mercy[13] we are simply saying to God: Lord, be to us as You are! Act toward us as You do! We want you to be with us and do with us as You Yourself are and actually do! . . . Mercy is at the heart of everything that God is and does.[14]

The gift and grace of all this process and faithfulness came many years later when I met the person who was once in leadership again. We met as though nothing had ever come between us. I don't know what work she did. I just know that my work freed me to be genuinely before her in loving-kindness. And for that I am grateful.

*I open myself*
*to another day of loving and life and being loved.*
*I open myself*
*to receive what births itself out of stillness.*
*I open myself*
*to the gracious coming of God.*

*– October 9, 1993*

---

13  Author's note: I prefer to use "Beloved One, have mercy."

14  Hopko, Thomas, *The Lenten Spring.* Readings for Great Lent (Crestwood N.Y St. Vladimir's Press 1983), 62.

# CHAPTER 17:
## Sacred Silence

## Sacred Silence is:

- A place of wordlessness that speaks to our heart and draws us into the breath of God.
- A place where stillness is like a gentle breeze that breathes upon our mind in open response to holy learning, holy wisdom, insight, healing, oneness.
- The interior space or place where God writes, whispers, and embraces us in the enough-ness of our creation.

## Sacred Silence is:

- The wordlessness that rests us so that we can emerge knowing something of being holy, being held by the holy.
- Unhurried, unpressured, in-pressed to evoke a song of soul that reverberates in the universe.
- Full. It can press against the womb of our heart that has the capacity to birth newness.
- The heartbeat of the universe where all is one, all is in communion with promise.
- An opening to the great tenderness and affection of sacred presence, and in it all, God is with us.

And I would say that in the place of Sacred Silence, in the wordless reality of God, dwells my uncreated self, my origin that became fashioned with matter.

There is no magic to finding silence, nor is it an act of will, but it is a reality of presence, being in presence, quieting the mind, stilling the body even if it is in walking. There are some I know who cannot sit in silence but can be in silence while they move their body. Others I know find silence in painting, quilting, being in nature, or are drawn into to it by listening to music. These mediums empty the mind, open the heart and spirit, and draw us into what is beyond our reason. Pascal once said that the heart has reasons that reason does not understand. As a Byzantine Poustinik, I practice the prayer of gazing. I gaze from this place of silence and hold the world—its joys, its suffering, its grief, its beauty—and I am still, wordless, at home in a place that only silence lives and speaks to my heart. It is a place that doesn't belong to me but a place where all of life meets in blessing the world.

*It is easy to pray when my heart is filled with gratitude.*
*It is easy to pray*
*when I have nothing more to do than sit*
*in this wonderful presence of love and be embraced by it.*
*All those who come to mind and heart,*
*that they too may be nourished*
*by this Sacred Silence and Holy Presence.*
*Resting in God, there are so many who come.*
*And I know*
*that in these sacred moments of meeting*
*the pain and joy of the whole universe is touched by the fragrance*
*that ensues.*
*And God comes . . .*
*God comes*
*and holds.*

*– October 10, 1995*

# CHAPTER 18:
## Seized by Wonder

## *The Essential Element of Wonder*

I strained to hear his words. "Sam," he said, "when I regained consciousness, my first feelings were not of despair or anger. I felt only gratitude to God for my life, for every moment I had lived. I was ready to depart. *Take me, O Lord*, I thought, *I have seen so many miracles in my lifetime*. He paused for a moment, then added: "I did not ask for success; I asked for wonder. And you gave it to me.[15]

> *Without wonder*
> *We can't rest in the heart of Sacred Consciousness*
> *Without suffering*
> *We can't know the tears of a grieving God.*
> *Without losing and finding,*
> *searching and waiting,*
> *dreaming and birthing*
> *we can't be held in the heart of love that draws us*
> *into the future*
> *that says BE! I AM with you in all things and in*
> *all ways.*
>
> *– January 2023*

And we hear the emergence of the eighty-four-year-old prophetess Anna, who had lived long in prayer and fasting, arriving at just the right moment to look upon the awaited one. She spoke of his future and his leadership toward liberation and transformation.[16] She strikes me as one filled with wonder, ready and awake in old age to unveil the invitation and gift of the future. Imagine growing old in wonder.

For me, wonder is such a significant gift of Holy Mystery, of Sacred Presence, of being embraced by Divine Grace. For me, Divine Grace is moving in the breath of God, being held and fed and invited to a deep consciousness of timelessness and Oneness. Moving in the breath of God can lead to God seizures, being filled with wonder, stopped by amazement. This opens up whole universes waiting to be explored and held. I believe wonder is an essential element of our

---

15  Hehschel, Abraham Joshua, *I Asked for Wonder: A Spiritual Anthology*, (1983), vii.

16  Luke 2:36-38.

original curiosity that sends us out to have life opened, unfolded to relationship, reverence, and falling in love again and again. It is an essential doorway to grace. It opens us (our humanity) to the tenderness and the gracious generosity of God's creative imagination and joy.

In a welcoming environment, we start our lives full of fascination and wonder. It bursts out of us, stops us in our tracks. It activates our curiosity and sends us to explore. Wonder and curiosity make us watchful, taking in what struck us, drawing us into learning and being available to the more, to what is beyond our immediate understanding. It draws us into being held by Sacred Presence where we find we live and move and breathe like a fish breathes in water. We become exposed to the reality that every particle in the universe is infused with Sacred Presence. Sacred Presence is the very breath of life that breathes in us, toward us, wrapping us in what evokes and stirs life to live. It is rarely far from us. It sits at the door of our wakefulness waiting in anticipation for relationship.

For example, did you know: There is research out of Australia that speaks of female fairy-wrens teaching their embryo chicks a password while still in their eggs, so that when they hatch they recognize the mother's call, and the parent can distinguish its own chick from the one belonging to the parasite bird. There is a brood of parasite Horsfield bronze-cuckoos, that lay eggs in the fairy-wren's nest, hoping that its chicks will be cared for by the fairy-wren. The Horsfield bronze-cuckoos produce begging calls that do not closely resemble the parental fairy-wren password; so the fairy-wrens distinguish their own chicks for feeding.[17]

When Mary, my companion in community, and I first moved to our house in New Westminster, B.C., we decided to put some birdhouses up on the side of our garage. We bought some beautiful ones made from cedar by one of the members of Cook's Ferry Indian

---

17  Colombelli-Négrel, D., Hauber, M. E., Robertson, J., Sulloway, F. J., Hoi, H., Griggio, M. and Kleindorfer, S. (2012). Embryonic learning of vocal To Beat a Parasite, Birds Teach Their Young a Secret Password. https://www.wired.com/2014/06.

Band. Mary and I tole-painted them, hung them, and hoped the chickadees might find one of them attractive. It was our first spring there and neither of us knew anything about chickadees so were delighted to find that one pair chose one of the houses. This house was hung over the brick walkway next to our garage. About three weeks in, activity around and in the birdhouse increased. Mary and I began to get up very early to watch and wait. I decided to pad the surrounding area on the walkway so that when the birds fledged, they wouldn't come crashing down and hurt themselves.

One fine, sunny day, the parents were in the cherry tree calling. Calling and feeding, calling and waiting. One little chickadee—it may have been one of the others in the nest too—kept coming to the hole, sometimes almost sitting on the edge, and popping back into the nest, coming back up, looking around, sitting and filling the hole with itself asking to be fed, while the parent in the cherry tree kept calling. Very quietly, I set up my camera and zoom lens; Mary set herself up to wait and watch on the deck. (Fortunately, our schedule for the day was pretty clear so that we could live this mystery in amazement and not have to leave and move onto something else.) Amazingly, the first little bird glided onto the lawn. No crash landing. It just sat and looked around. Then worked at flight. Big learning, I would say, spreading its wings and landing a short distance still on the grass. It was calling to be fed, but no parent came to the rescue at this point. The parents were still focused on the remaining ones in the birdhouse. And then the magic began in the backyard. The hummingbird came to feed on the flowers, finches came with their young and sat on the fence nearby. The baby chickadee made its way to a little stone ledge by the grapevines, still calling to be fed. And to our amazement a young finch came and joined the baby and began to feed it. The backyard began to resonate with an amazing energy of life and a chorus of singing birds. It was as though they all congregated to encourage the remaining two chickadees to find the courage to leave and to fly. It was four hours before the next little one fledged. I think all of creation cheered in that moment. The last little bird took its time too. It would come to the hole, sit, look around, the parent would call, feed it on the fly, and go back to calling. And the magic of the intense presence remained. It was as if God, the creator of all, danced in our garden that day. Now, each year we sit and wait, arriving early in the morning on some days when the signs are there of readiness, or we sit in the backyard under the cherry tree, or sit in the sunroom where friends have joined us to watch and wait, drink coffee in silence, and hold the sacred moments of emergence in wonder and awe. These moments of reality are a privilege. We aren't necessary for these moments to live. These fledglings would take place without us, as they do in the neighbouring hedge lining our fence. But that we can be present, that these little magnificent creatures go about their work in our presence when we are in the yard is pure gift in grace.

Wonder for me is central to the creative expression of sacredness. Beatrice Bruteau speaks of God's ecstasy as God spilling God's self out creatively, calling each one of us and all that lives to become who and what we are contributing to the emergence within the universe. She says, "The highest, best, most perfect way to be a Creator is to create a self-creating world. This most satisfyingly fulfills the Creator because it most thoroughly incarnates the self-givingness of the Creator."[18]

Wonder moves us to joy. Joy moves us to seeing and hearing what is both visible and invisible. Breathing and moving in this grace keeps us full of spirit and generosity. Wonder keeps us eternally young, alive in our spirit, aware that in fact we age, our bodies become old and frail, and we go back to the earth from which we have come. But our life, the grace and consciousness from which we have emerged, continues in the mystery that draws us ever onward in cooperation with the fashioning of what is not-yet. I believe we will know life beyond the veil; it is only a breath away. I believe that wonder is the first gaze placed on us by the One who fashioned us and called us into being and out of which we have been sent. It is to receive this gaze again and again so that we mature into a radiance of

---

18 Bruteau, Beatrice. God's Ecstasy: The Creation of a Self-Creating World. (The United States of America, The Crossroad Publishing Company, 1997), p.44

what resonates in the deepest recesses of our being. Wonder allows us to see and meet the mystery in creation, it leads us to continue to find the newness in others who are part of the woven relationships that call us forth and send us into tolerance and acceptance of differences. Wonder is the ever-present mystery that emanates Sacred Presence, drawing us to the unveiling of youthfulness, wisdom, and the eternal spirit in us that never dies. To not avail ourselves to wonder, to not sit at the edge of amazement, allows for the option of shrivelling up interiorly and dying without having lived.

So let us sit and watch the beauty and mystery of sunsets, resting in Sacred Presence, practicing the prayer of gazing. Let us avail ourselves to the invitation of beauty in trees and flowers opening into blossom, preparing their sweetness for the pollinators. Let us sit at the edge of our gardens, or rest on our knees, if they still allow us, to watch and welcome the fruit of the earth in the gift of vegetables. Let us create space for wonder and mystery and gather these moments in gratitude at the end of a day.

We carry a wondering that goes with the ego, that questions and ponders and carries curiosity. There is also being amazed, which is not the same as wonder. It is kind of the first step. Amazement carries surprise, tends to stop us in our tracks, and can lead us to some form of analysis. Wonder, on the other hand, fills our hearts and spirits with a sense of fullness, of wordlessness, joy, and stillness. For me it is an expansiveness of my inner being and can bring me to tears or a deep stillness that holds me beyond words, that can explain or describe what is voiceless word and pure gift.

A story: In the mid '90s, Mary and I did a two-year discernment to see if we were meant to share a ministry of welcome together. I began to do work in B.C. on a more regular basis. I commuted between Winnipeg and the lower mainland and I continued to accompany people in Winnipeg until they were ready to send me to BC. I sold my house in Winnipeg, and stayed with friends who had an old black cat named Paws. When I would arrive at their house, Paws met me at the door, and led me downstairs to the room I used. Sometimes I would find her sleeping on a cupboard shelf in my room but most often in her chair in the adjoining room where I received people. One day I was asked to meet with someone I had never met before (Paws was in her chair, asleep). As the woman began to share her story with me, she touched into a pocket of pain and began to sob. As I sat and listened and received, Paws got up out of her chair, came to the sofa where the woman sat and wept, and fully stretched her front paws up onto the arm of the sofa. I looked at Paws, fully stretched, fully focused on the weeping woman. She stayed like that, not taking her eyes off her, until the woman passed through the pain. She then got down, stretched on a pillar made specially for her, and went back to her chair. I found myself utterly amazed. I had never had such an experience with a cat, or any other animal actually. At the end of that day, as I gathered my learnings and my gratitudes, I found myself filled with wonder and a sense of curiosity. My amazement, my intellectual wondering asked, "How can this be?" Is it possible that compassion is carried beyond humanity and is part of other living creatures? For me this is another pause and reflection in Sacred Presence, a potential path to holiness.

# CHAPTER 19:
## Curiosity: A Leading Thread of Creation

IN HER BOOK Madeleine L'Engle wrote: "Not so long ago the redeemed Hubble telescope detected fifty billion hitherto undiscovered galaxies in a slice of space no bigger than a grain of rice. Awesome!"[19]

In the Amplified Bible there is word I like: Selah, which means pause and reflect on that! That is the invitation of curiosity. Pause and reflect on that.

---

19   L'Engle Madeleine, *Bright Evening Star: Mystery Of The Incarnation* (Kelowna B.C. Canada: Northstone Publishing, 1997), 101.

Dorothee Soelle wrote: "I think that every discovery of the world plunges us into jubilation, a radical amazement that tears apart the veil of triviality. Nothing is to be taken for granted, least of all beauty."[20]

If the Creator, Sacred Consciousness, God, Great Spirit, imagines possibilities, empowers creation to continue welcoming the future through creativity, then curiosity is another essential element related to wonder. We need to develop a healthy curiosity that nourishes our personal emergence and invites the emergence within community and society. There are different expressions of curiosity. There is the curiosity that likes to keep an eye on a neighbour to see what is happening, or who is visiting now. There is the curiosity that sometimes is expressed through what can feel like interrogation, wanting all the news of a person's life. There is the curiosity of science, philosophy, psychology, biblical studies. The gift and power of curiosity can either help or limit our learning, depending on where it leads us. Curiosity is not simply asking questions, it is sitting in the questions, resting in questions, and waiting for revelation.

I once lived in an area where the Hell's Angels lived across the street from me. When I would sit on the balcony having my morning coffee, I would watch the comings and the goings and made up all kinds of scenarios in my head. Occasionally I would see someone come wearing the colours on their leather jacket. One time a helicopter even landed in the front yard. Another time four police cars arrived, and two of the residents were driven away. I had a field day with that. Perhaps you have noticed yourself doing what I did? If you don't have all the information, you make it up. Our brain needs to link things together. It may be as simple as seeing someone frowning, crying, or sitting in a car at the side of the road. This form of wondering satisfies something of our curiosity, and we go on.

But our curiosity is much more valuable than that. It is not only essential for stringing ideas together, but it also fuels our creativity,

---

20   Soelle, Dorothee. *The Silent Cry: Mysticism and* Resistence, (Minneapolis, MN Augsburg Fortress, 2001), 89.

and it is the beginning of our wonder as mentioned before. We need to learn to discipline our curiosity. Where do we exercise our curiosity? Sometimes my curiosity is piqued in relation to someone's life, and I say to myself that it is not my business. If they want me to know, they will tell me. I have a phrase that I use and some of my friends have adopted: "It's none of my business, but I'd really like to know." It's my call to discipline curiosity.

I like to invite people to become aware of what attracts them in nature. What books do they spend their time reading, and what does that answer in them? There is a book by Beatrice Bruteau I have been reading on and off for five years called *The Holy Thursday Revolution*. When I first began to struggle my way through it, a friend who was here on retreat and rest asked, "Why are you reading it if it is such a challenge?" I said, "Because it is leading me into the new, and into another perspective that I haven't explored, and uses a language that is new to me. So, for me, it is worth the struggle and will enlarge who I am and how I see." One specific statement I carry with me from the book is: "You are not my other self; you are my self." Now when I receive Eucharist, I look at all those who are receiving. Then when I leave the liturgy, I reflect on all of the colours and nationalities that have become a part of my body because we are one.

I ask those I accompany what relationships in their lives are life-giving, and how do they nourish their lives? What kinds of realities bring joy or are boring but are chosen, because it is the kind thing to do in some situations? I recently went to see the stage play *Shrek* because a mother and her ten-year-old wanted me to go with them. I enjoyed their company, and I was really impressed with the quality of acting and extraordinary voices in these high school students. I chose to go because my young friend really wanted me to. I would not normally have chosen to go because I had seen the Shrek DVD multiple times with my young friends who came to visit. And because I had seen the movie multiple times, I didn't carry a great deal of curiosity to see the play, none-the-less I was glad I went. I appreciated the delight of my young friend and the audience.

Wonder is at the heart of mysticism. Curiosity explores how to break it open. Wonder is resting in the fullness of soul. Curiosity is walking around the interior reality so that it can be shared. I love chasing sunsets. But I have no words for them, so to share them with someone, I have to bring that person with me; then we can be in awe and wordlessness together. If that's not realistic and possible, I show them my photographs. It's still not the same, but it allows for the exercise of imagination and memory.

# CHAPTER 20:
## Gratitude

## The Essential Element of Gratitude

*The universe is infused with grace.*
*It greets me at every turn,*
*full of invitation*
*to grow free and*
*to choose life.*
*Often what is necessary can seem so simple.*
*Sometimes so difficult.*
*To greet the day with a grateful heart.*
*To carry an openness so that I can receive*
*all—*
*only that is required.*
*God's desire for me is full.*
*My humanity resonates with divine desire.*
*All I need is the disposition to respond.*

*– April 10, 2001*

All my life I have carried a great tendency to be overwhelmed by gratitude. It may be activated by something that happened in relationship, it may be a consequence of prayer, feeling filled by the amazing presence of grace experiencing God's active presence and love acting in the life of another, or in my own. I have seen so many extraordinary expressions of God, Sacred Presence, living and acting in healing, in insight given and revelation of awesome mystery. I have been present to people experiencing incremental physical healing through prayer, through counselling, through journaling.

Gratitude was/is one of the essential attributes, ingredients of soul, that empowered me to find my way to the other side of moments in my life. It fashioned my consciousness of goodness and beauty around me. It fashioned my ability to endure different forms and levels of suffering: suffering of the heart, of the body, of relationships, of loneliness, of loss. Gratitude drew me into deep moments of immersion in beauty and goodness, in people, in nature, in books, in photography, in music. At times I sang and danced through my inner pain. I wrote music to express what impacted me. It all wrapped me in the sacred, in the God I was coming to know, the Uncontainable One and the available holy mystery of Sacred Presence.

Gratitude and praise empower us and the universe. We cannot be grateful and bitter at the same time. It is our work to find what stands in the way of our gratitude, what prevents us from being a celebrating presence in our homes, our communities, our world. It is this that helps me build pockets of non-violence. It is to this that my life is directed as a woman of God among others.

*Gratitude comes to consciousness through moments of quiet gazing*
*into the heart.*
*Gratitude comes when in the stillness I hear the footsteps*
*of my beloved entering the space of my listening.*
*Gratitude comes when the sky opens and soft gentle rains water the*
*thirsting earth.*
*Gratitude comes when the waiting in my longing has found*
*a response.*
*Gratitude comes when light is given to open the unseeing of*
*my search,*
*and the unhearing of my heart when confusion fills me,*
*and I feel abandoned or lost . . . even for the moment.*
*Gratitude comes in the gentle touch of gifting through a look, a meal,*
*a letter, a word.*
*Gratitude comes when I allow myself to be held as gifted and giver,*
*as given as one created for love in the world.*

*– September 1995*

Gratitude is an interior stance that houses such feelings as joy, wonder, awe, availability to the other, to prayer, to peace, to vulnerability. Gratitude avails us to the presence of love. Gratitude is one point where the Byzantine Poustinik bows in profound adoration before the Holy One of abundant generosity and gift, the One who knows no bounds in loving, or forgiveness. Gratitude is a prayer of praise that resonates and opens life and the world to the healing gaze of God whose tenderness melts the hardened heart and opens and transforms because there is room for that. Developing a practice of gathering gratitude stirs our awareness, affirms our existence, and empowers us to receive even the smallest gestures that reach toward us as embrace, and gives light to any form of darkness that tempts to leave us discouraged.

*My soul trembles and my body weeps.*
*Holy are you, O God.*
*I praise your Holy Name with all the Names uttered that name*
*you Holy.*
*My soul trembles and my body weeps before your awesome presence.*
*I am filled with love, held in love, and I am in love with you, my God.*
*I am thankful that you have given yourself alive within creation. I am*
*thankful for your self- revelation in Jesus.*
*I am thankful for your promise to be with me in all things and in*
*all ways.*

*– October 10, 1993*

# CHAPTER 21:
## Service: The Unveiling and Actualizing of Gifts

OUR LIVES ARE not for ourselves. The reign of God, the companionship of empowerment, is about being immersed in the sacredness of the divine imagination out of which we have come, and engage in the emergence of grace, in love of justice, of truth, and a commitment to wholeness. We learn to read our interior movements, our reactions. We learn to filter our feelings to see what is rooted in the past that magnifies our present perception and find what we are meant to respond to, address, let be, or ignore. Our feelings are our feelings, they can tell us a part of the truth, but not the whole truth.

We honour them without letting them lead the whole of our lives, because sometimes unprocessed they can lead us to choose what is not of life. Other times, our whole body is moved to stop, the body knowing there is something we need to take notice of. So, what is there in the feelings? What am I meant to know, be aware of? Sometimes the stop comes as a warning, being in the presence of untruth, or danger. We take heed of, and we process this as soon as possible so that we can be responsive rather than reactive. We stay in charge of our lives that way rather than giving our lives over to another, or a situation. Being in charge is not about controlling but standing in an inner place of authority.

> *The invitation to do and to believe. At times to make sacrifice, but one that empowers life, that enables relationship and mutuality, that brings forth right relations. All this opens our eyes, moves us to consciousness of self and others. In this there is no self-abuse or the abuse of others. There are times when the necessary choice for life involves putting ourselves aside for another. It may not be something that "I" really "want" to do, but listening inside, it is something I am being asked to do because life requires it. And as I listen and discern inside myself, I know I have what I need to respond. I have what I need to show up for the life of another, for justice and truth. I/we are invited to stand well in our freedom and strength, take our full stature in the companionship of empowerment. We carry within us the freedom to become who we are, to live in harmony, compassion, mercy, available to transformation, community, mutual relationships. We are well made and made for this time.*

> – February 18, 2000

On September 7, 1993, as I reflected on the months since Joan's death, I found myself at another crossroad and in need of discernment. I asked myself, "What am I meant to do with the rest of my life?" And in the light of that, and my inner mandate to live love to the fullest: "What does it mean for me to be giving right to the end of my giving? What is required of my self-knowledge, and of my commitment to this life journey?" In my young days it meant to give and give and give, ask nothing in return, and give again. Forget about yourself, just give without question, and often times whether it was needed or not, asked for or not. Giving indiscriminately was understood as an abundance of generosity. I understood it as a sign of being deeply loving. There is another question that is required when looking at this question: "From where in me do I give?" What is the interior structure, the carrying place of intention, that is activated? Is it a response, a reaction, a need to do, an obligation, an invitation, or is it a desire to look good before others? And what of this is it a part of one's own nature, a generosity of heart and mind and spirit? It isn't my intention to be judgemental or critical in asking these questions. It is to be reflective. My mind has to be in my heart to recognize its shifts into revelation. For me, in service, as in prayer, I choose to place my head in my heart, to be led, taught, opened, transformed, and sent.

We are born out of a generous spirit; it is one of the essential attributes of our nature. When we are children, we are encouraged to develop that reality in us, and it helps us develop an awareness of others, and as we age to share who we are so that life, creation, the reality of Sacred Mystery can continue to emerge in us and around us.

I have a young friend who came for a visit once when she was three. As we sat in the backyard, she asked if she could pick some grapes from the grapevine. I said, "Sure, you are welcome to them."

Off she went and came back with a handful, her little hand about the size of my palm. She sat beside me and before she took one for herself, she offered me one.

I said, "No, you enjoy them."

"Here, Doreen, try one," she insisted.

So I did, and then she had one. Then she said, "Try another one," and so it went.

She as a three-year-old was already aware of life beyond herself. Already learning to give and to love in these gracious moments of her life.

And so, to give to the end of our giving, to love to the end of our love, is to be rooted in generosity, grounded in love, and living in a deep freedom so that what is given, how one loves is whole, in this moment, in this time and in this day. Tomorrow may offer another opportunity to exercise this grace. We simply are asked to be available to it. I would like to say that consciousness was before all creation existed. Consciousness, spirit, was all there was. But until spirit entered matter, it was powerless. Until consciousness became relationship with all that is, there was no emergence.

> *And for us without reflection, awareness, conscious-*
> *ness, we don't mature, become who we are. We grow*
> *old and wither without relationships, we remain a*
> *living bud without unfolding, waiting for life to come*
> *to us. I remember Joan's father. He had a third-grade*
> *education. He was a farmer, a man of the earth. He*
> *was in relationship with so much life. When he would*
> *drive into the yard and the cattle heard his voice, they*
> *would come running toward him. When I occasion-*
> *ally helped him clean the barn, we would lean on our*
> *shovels and he would tell me about the cattle, where*
> *the meadowlarks were nesting, and how to be watch-*
> *ful when walking in the pasture. We emerge, mature*
> *through reflection and relationship.*

– August 6, 2001

As we are actualizing our gifts, as we come to know and accept in ourselves what brings meaning and the sense of wholeness in ourselves, we contribute to the emergence of life around us, in our relationships, community, and society. This self-emergence carries a wakefulness to what brings life, what is missing that can be invited to birth, be put in place for life to flourish. Some of us recognize the absence of justice and are called to work for it. Others recognize what is necessary for the healing of heart and mind and work to facilitate what is needed for its healing. When each of us brings the fruit of our history, its gift of learning through our own healing, the gift of our own wounding, we bring forth the capacity to assist in the healing of others. The gift of the gospel calls us to liberate the whole of life, where no one is left behind, where all of creation is honoured in its effort to emerge as grace and blessing. The mission of Jesus was about bringing into reality this dream of the possible within community. It is what the empowerment of companionship, also known as the reign of God, is meant to become.

Recently, Mary and I were visiting a home on Hornby Island. There we met a young couple who were also doing a drop-in. As we left to descend some stairs that had no handrails, I asked Mary to go ahead of me so that I could use her shoulder for support as well as my walking stick, because the three stairs were precarious. I felt a hand slip under my elbow and a hand on my back guiding me down. It was very brief, this action. It was the young man we'd just met, who had just followed his nature to care. I met him again the next day, and we had conversation around his attentiveness. There are gifts that we carry that are very natural to us. These we often don't take seriously. I hear people say, "Oh, it's nothing, just what I do." But it matters because it is part of our nature, our attentiveness to life.

The magnolia tree on my street puts forth its blossoms first, filling the street with beauty, and then as it lets go of the flowers, the leaves emerge, bringing oxygen and shade and the gift of green to the street. It is the nature of the magnolia tree to awaken our wonder, to offer its shade and photosynthesis.

Each culture, each religion, each tradition has the capacity to bring wholeness, gift, grace to bless and offer a path of wholeness and relationship.

Service is not about being a do-gooder but responding to the impulse of life that carries the invitation for emergence. That is the gift of aging, of reflection, of the gift of prayer, the gift of relationship and the gift of differences lived as offering. The creative imagination of Sacred Consciousness, Sacred Presence, the genius of the Creator that I know as God, as Wisdom, as Spirit, is abundant in generosity and possibility. This sacred knowing and desire has room for all of creation to respond. Service moves toward putting something of life in place. It is about dreaming the possible and helping it happen. It is about embodying care, love, compassion, living justice, truth, showing mercy. It is challenging systems, laying down one's life when necessary, so that another can live or have what they need to live. It is trusting that each of us is well made and invited to bring forth the fullness of who we are so that the best in us, the best in life, has an opportunity to move toward wholeness. In all of that is holiness, broken open, blessed, and given for the life of the world. We each are a profound consequence of sacred imagination, holy delight. I invite you to be open to receive. You are meant for this time, as I know I am.

*Gracious God,*
*My heart awaits you.*
*Over and over again,*
*I lean my heart against your womb,*
*listening as it throbs with life and light*
*and vibrates with infinite love and direction.*
*You stir my longings and my desire and my passions*
*toward a life full of knowing wisdom*
*that unveils and births the longing of the universe.*
*Passionate God, seize my longings, enflame my passions,*
*make soul through my woman knowing.*

*– June 1995*

# CHAPTER 22:
## Be a Mystic in the Ordinary

THE MYSTIC IS one who is fueled by awe and wonder and fired by compassion and holy justice. Prayer and contemplation are the pathway of the mystic who comes to be in relationship with the holy, the intimate breath of Sacred Presence, in the gift and grace of all creation and humanity.

## Become a Mystic in the Ordinary

*Become mystics in the ordinary . . .*

*Become aware of God in and through every breath of your body . . . and know the grace of Sacred Presence.*

*Holiness isn't an illusion. It is a body, a soul, a heart, a mind, that is a container for grace.*

*A bearer of good and graciousness. A presence steeped in reflective truth . . . a voice unsheltered from the wind so that it can be carried to depths waiting to be recognized and named.*

*Become aware of God in and through the breath of your body . . .*

*And let the stillness come and lead you, draw you . . .*

*For holiness is your nature.*

*And you will find that God comes because God is holy and has bent into creation with the*

*greatest of reverence and tenderness.*

*You will find that God comes because life is fragile and meant to be held*

*and affirmed and made strong*

*to cease the doubt that we are good and cherished.*

*You will find that God comes because relationship is God's nature.*

*And relationship carries the reflection of our soul and our respect for the one who is before us*

*and draws us toward completion.*

*God lives between us as carefully as the air that surrounds us.*

*God is Sacred Presence.*

*Become mystics in the ordinary.*

*Be in a shopping centre and allow yourself to be held by the gaze of a child who only*

*knows how to seize you through their innocence.*

*Be in a parade and allow your own childlikeness to release joy into*
*a crowd of strangers.*
*Be in a garden and be tamed by a rose.*
*Rest in silence and let the stillness unveil its sacred to you.*
*Become mystics in the ordinary and hesitate only long enough to be*
*named by the caress of*
*God's face raising love-light over you.*
*And then continue on your journey toward your nature*
*and holiness will find you.*

*– September 16, 1995*

## Naming Gifts, Qualities, Attributes

How do we name the reflection of the Sacred Image living in us, how is it lived out of us? There is a radiance that emanates through this lived reality in us. People are attracted to it and reach toward it or like to sit in is presence as it shines forth. St. Paul speaks of us as saints. There are many I have come to know and would name saints. Find some in your life. They are wonderful to hang out with.

Take a moment now and then and look deeply into your own eyes. If it is morning, say, "Good morning, beloved of God!" Look into the divine image in you, what do you see? In the Christian scriptures, "Do not be afraid" is used 365 times. Somebody counted them, and I believed him. Look and see the wonder of the creation you carry and are invited to become.

The saint is one who is able to live in the ordinariness of the present and maintain peace.

And I would maintain that we have idealized this reality and placed holiness at the disposal of the very few. Holiness is about the incarnation of the divine unbound from within.

## A Reflection on Being a Saint

*A saint is born out of reality, not out of some isolated point on the*
*horizon where everything looks new . . .*

151

*They emerge out of the breath of struggle and pain and bleeding . . .*
*And discover that they can stand and survive . . . and find blessing*
*and birth and more struggle, because that's how life is.*
*I lived with a saint once . . .*
*Fresh with life and old in wonder . . .*
*Marked by anger and wounded by doubt.*
*She grew beyond it to a place where love and truth were friends.*
*She wasn't perfect in the way we would want people to be . . . with no*
*glitches or warts or cracks . . .*
*She just was fair and whole and honest and full of love and gratitude*
*. . . even if she was impatient at times . . .*
*But I know she was a saint because she loved mornings.*
*She loved the sound of birds and butterflies and falling snow.*
*And she could live with me and let me be . . . that's important, you*
*know, when you're as human as I am, filled with intensity and*
*dreams and so many ways of being in a day.*
*Yes, saints are born out of reality, because they choose to stay with the*
*struggle rather than escape. They choose to reach into love rather than*
*hide in resentment and bitterness and not coming to know the other*
*side of what brought them to that point in the first place.*
*I think I'd like to be a saint someday . . .*
*Maybe if I pause enough in the mornings . . .*
*And don't mind waiting in shopping lines . . . as if I could get through*
*all that needs to be done in a day . . .*
*Maybe if I embrace the pain and the struggle and the bleeding long*
*enough to find the gift and blessing it holds . . .*
*Maybe if I would just be glad to be a human in process of receiving*
*and growing and giving and being led to know, rather than having to*
*have everything in place on the first shot . . .*
*Maybe if I stay with the struggle long enough with my eyes and ears*
*and heart open . . .*
*And give birth and am born in this moment rather than in some*
*unsuspecting hope of tomorrow . . .*
*I could be a saint, you know, if I be all that I could be in this now that*
*I am . . .*

*Yes, I just need to breathe and hold the moment in enough softness .*
*. . and reality gets changed into the real . . . and a saint is born for a*
*moment at least.*

*– April 2, 1995*

## Reflecting on How You are Made

How would you name your gifts, qualities, attributes? List them individually on a piece of paper. If it feels a little strange, use your non-dominant hand. (Amazing things surface using our non-dominant hand. People have met their inner poet doing that.) Where and how do you find yourself exercising them? What evidence do you have of their emergence and expression? Write them in your journal. Staying in your head and just thinking about them doesn't encourage you to own them. Let them take hold of you.

Take your list, cut each gift and attribute into individual pieces, and place them in a basket, a bowl, or whatever, and choose one each day and watch for its expression. It's like giving that gift of water or sunlight that allows it to root more deeply in you. Sometimes we see the gift exercised only as an inkling, almost at the edge of our awareness. As we catch its expression, as we allow it to emerge in us, it becomes a gift to the world in and through us. Sometimes it is so much a part of us that we haven't noticed it, but others may have acknowledged it, and we just let it pass without hearing it because we may not find it very significant. We offer responses like, "Oh, it's nothing," or, "It's just natural." When people affirm some reality in us, check it out by asking: "What of this is true of me?" If it is true, receive it. If not, then work with it so that you claim what of it is true. This is not about feel-good stuff. It's about owning the truth about what we are made of, what blessing we carry, what within us contributes to the solidity of who we are.

When we live our giftedness, we leave a deposit in our stead. Our gifts call us into mission, and they are often called out of us in community, sometimes challenging us to believe in ourselves in whole new ways. I have come to know that I am a daughter of sacredness, and my work is to be at one with Woman/Mother God/Wisdom. My integration, my wholeness, lies in recapturing the image that had been lost to me because of hurts, comparisons, others' judgements, my self-hatred and self-rejection, and whatever else challenged me to not take seriously that I am a gift, fashioned from love, to be love. And so, I continue to take the risk to journey to the edge of language and ideas and delve into Eternal Presence, steeped in "Radiant Energy,"[21] to be woman: a full human being.

## *Examination of Consciousness*[22]

Journaling is both a tool and a companion. It opens up the inner universe, helps put relationships and interactions into perspective, affirms our searching, and allows us to learn how to read our inner way and language.

Examination of consciousness: In looking at the following, what do you find yourself attracted to, drawn to, that can deepen your relationship to Holy Mystery and to yourself? Respond, journal around what draws you to deepen and own as your life in this day.

1. **Upon waking:**

   Learn to be attentive to any dreams that you may have had. Note them. Write as many details as you can. How did you feel in the dream? In waking? What, who is familiar? Not? What question does your dream pose for you, what invitation?

2. **In looking toward this day:**

   What do I hope for, anticipate, desire?
   What needs to be, or is necessary, to be in place for me, to have what I want, desire?

---

21  Bruteau, Beatrice. *God's Ecstasy: The Creation of a Self-Creating World* (The United States of America, The Crossroad Publishing Company, 1997), 28

22  Kostynuik, Doreen. Examination of Consciousness (Winnipeg 1992, revision 2000)

What needs to be, or is necessary, to be in place in myself? What needs to be, or is necessary, to be in place in relation to the situations facing me? Are there some things that feel challenging to me? What can I rely on in myself to meet these challenges? Is there something that I might need to let go of? If I choose to do what I can, no more and no less, what would that mean for me?

3. **Evening:**

What lives in me as I look back on this day?
Is there anything that draws my attention that would be good for me to explore and have more light on? If so, what? What learnings does this offer me?
How would I name the areas to which I gave my life today? How does that make me feel? What learnings does this offer me?
Was I aware of Sacred Presence in any of the moments of my day? How would I name, describe this? What grace did this allow me to receive, be aware of? Through whom or what did this come? Would I say that I was led to gratitude, insight, knowing? If so, gather these. What does this allow me to know in this point of my journey?

4. **Closing:**

Be still before the Holy One who names you again as beloved. Breathe in and out gently. Rest in Sacred Presence.

### And God Slid

*God poured God-Self into creation*
*And the God of Power disappeared to be unveiled in Love.*
*Be awake! Love beckons—lives in all, in you, in me!*
*Be awake then, so that you can recognize and follow.*
*Recognize and be made strong!*
*Recognize and be made firm!*
*The God of Power has disappeared into illusions and rigidity.*
*Self-revealing sacredness lives in all creation, here and into the stars.*

155

*Be awake to receive.*
*Be awake to respond.*
*Be awake to be Love.*
*It is who you are, who I Am.*

*– October 5, 2017*


*Go gently but firmly in this journey.*
*I wish you much grace and blessings.*

*– Doreen D. Kostynuik*

# ACKNOWLEDGEMENTS

MY DEEP GRATITUDE to Sr. Mary Beth McCurdy SCIC, who has encouraged and celebrated my writing for years, and to her congregation, the Sisters of Charity of the Immaculate Conception, who have partially funded the publishing of this work.

To the readers and editing helpers: Marietta and Johan Wouterloot, Cathy Hardy, Sr. Carolyn Osiek RSCJ, Charlene deFaye, Susan Hay, my first reader who waded through the first and final draft, and Mary Boucher who listened to every word again and again. I thank so many who, over the years, have awaited and encouraged the emergence of this book. I am very grateful to all who have believed in me and wanted to hear my life story and how it has formed me to become a listener of the heart. Finally, my thanks to FriesenPress for this launch.

Printed in the USA
CPSIA information can be obtained
at www.ICGtesting.com
JSHW011425040224
56377JS00025B/35

9 781039 189744